UNIVERSITIES AND ECONOMIC DEVELOPMENT IN AFRICA
Pact, academic core and coordination
SYNTHESIS REPORT

Nico Cloete, Tracy Bailey and Peter Maassen

Published by African Minds for the Centre for Higher Education Transformation (CHET),
House Vincent, First Floor, 10 Brodie Road, Wynberg Mews, Wynberg, 7800
Telephone: +27(0)21 763-7100 | Fax: +27(0)21 763-7117
E-mail: chet@chet.org.za | www.chet.org.za

© CHET 2011

ISBN 978-1-920355-80-7

E-book editions:
Ebrary 978-1-920355-81-4
MyiLibrary 978-1-920355-82-1
Adobe Digital Edition 978-1-920355-83-8

Produced by COMPRESS.dsl | www.compressdsl.com

Cover illustration by Raymond Oberholzer

Distributed by African Minds
4 Eccleston Place, Somerset West, 7130, South Africa
info@africanminds.co.za
www.africanminds.co.za

For orders from outside Africa, excluding North America:
African Books Collective
orders@africanbookscollective.com
www.africanbookscollective.com

For orders from North America:
Michigan State University Press
msupress@msu.edu
http://msupress.msu.edu/

Contents

Tables, figures and boxes   v

About this report   vii

A note about the data timeframe   viii

Acknowledgements   ix

The project group   xi

Acronyms and abbreviations   xiii

Executive summary   xv

CHAPTER 1: Introduction   1

1.1 Contextualising the project: The relationship between higher education and development   1

    1.1.1   International trends   1

    1.1.2   The African context   2

    1.1.3   The focus of prior research   5

1.2 Project focus and methodology   7

1.3 Analytical starting points for the study   9

    1.3.1   What the project is not doing   11

CHAPTER 2: Universities and economic development: Evidence of a pact?   13

2.1 The role of knowledge and universities in development   14

    2.1.1   A role for knowledge and universities in national and institutional policies and plans   14

    2.1.2   Notions about the role of knowledge and universities   17

CHAPTER 3: The academic core of eight African universities   23

3.1 Methodology   24

3.2 The academic core data   26

3.3 The strength of and changes in the academic core   29

3.4 Disjunctures between capacity and productivity   31

CHAPTER 4: Coordination and connectedness 37

4.1 Coordination and implementation of knowledge policies 38

    4.1.1 National coordination 38

    4.1.2 Implementation 42

4.2 University connectedness to external stakeholders 46

    4.2.1 Industry and community 46

    4.2.2 Foreign donors 48

4.3 The connectedness of development activities to the academic core 52

    4.3.1 Methodology 52

    4.3.2 The project data and analysis 53

    4.3.3 Discussion 57

CHAPTER 5: Conclusions and some implications 59

5.1 Pact needed on 'engine for development' role for universities 60

5.2 Strengthening the academic core – incentives are key 61

5.3 Coordination and connectedness to development 64

List of sources 68

Appendix A: A higher education and development profile of the countries 71

Appendix B: List of interviewees 75

Appendix C: Indicators of pact, coordination and implementation 79

Appendix D: Problems in collecting academic core data 81

Appendix E: Academic core indicators and ratings 82

Tables, figures and boxes

Tables

Table 1   Role for knowledge and universities in development   15

Table 2   National and institutional notions of the role of the university in
development   19

Table 3   Academic core indicators: Scores and changes (2001–2007)   27

Table 4   Academic core indicators: Ratings per university   28

Table 5   Academic core indicators: Average annual growth rates (2001–2007)   29

Table 6   Coordination of knowledge policies   39

Table 7   Implementation of knowledge policies and activities   42

Table 8   Overview of the development-related projects/centres   54

Table 9   Development projects/centres: 'Articulation' and 'strengthening the
academic core' ratings   55

Table A1   Gross domestic product (GDP) per capita vs. Human Development
Index (HDI)   72

Table A2   Selected higher education and economic development indicators   74

Table C1   A role for knowledge and universities in development   79

Table C2   Coordination and implementation   80

Table E1   Academic core indicators measurements and ratings   82

Figures

Figure 1   The four notions of the role of knowledge and universities in development   18

Figure 2   Academic core indicators (standardised data): Three selected universities   32

Figure 3   Plotting the development activities   56

Figure 4   The dynamics of the relationship between the pact, academic core and
coordination / connectedness   67

Boxes

Box 1   The knowledge economy and role of higher education in national and
institutional policies and plans   16

Box 2   Selected narratives on the role of the university in development   21

Box 3   Coordination of knowledge policies and activities   40

Box 4   Implementation of knowledge policies and activities   43

Box 5   Implementation of knowledge policies at institutional level   44

Box 6   University connectedness to external groupings   47

Box 7   Connecting internal university and external donor interests   51

About this report

This report synthesises the data and main findings of the eight African case studies which formed part of the HERANA Higher Education and Economic Development research programme. Other publications in the series include:

Higher education and economic development: A literature review

By Pundy Pillay (2010)

> This report reviews the international literature on the relationship between higher education and economic development. The review focuses on previous research and theory on the link between higher education and economic growth, the knowledge economy, innovation, and local and regional development. The review would be of interest to academics and students who work in the field of higher education studies.

Linking higher education and economic development: Implications for Africa from three successful systems

By Pundy Pillay (2010)

> This book synthesises the findings of case studies of three systems – Finland, South Korea and North Carolina in the US – that have successfully linked higher education to their economic development initiatives. This publication would be of particular interest to policy-makers and funders.

Universities and economic development in Africa: Country and university case studies

By Tracy Bailey, Nico Cloete and Pundy Pillay (2010)

> Eight country and university case studies – Botswana / University of Botswana; Ghana / University of Ghana; Kenya / University of Nairobi; Mauritius / University of Mauritius; Mozambique / Eduardo Mondlane University; South Africa / Nelson Mandela Metropolitan University; Tanzania / University of Dar es Salaam; Uganda / Makerere University.

> These reports provide the detailed evidence of the case studies of eight African countries and universities, focusing on national policy and coordination, as well as detailed information about the universities in the sample. These reports would be of particular interest to university leadership, as well as national policy-makers.

Academic publications

> Drawing on the above-mentioned reports and publications, we are also in the process of preparing three academic articles for publication in peer-reviewed journals as well as a chapter in a book.

A note about the data timeframe

This synthesis report and its associated case study reports were written in 2010 and published in early 2011. It should be noted that the data on which these reports are based ranges from 2001–2009. In particular, the academic core data cover the period 2001–2007, while the national and institutional policies, plans and project information is based on data collected in 2009.

Acknowledgements

During the post-independence period, every African country has struggled with the vexing issue of the role of higher education in development. While many studies on higher education in Africa deal with this problematic indirectly, very few have actually taken it on directly. It took a consultation and discussion period of almost three years between the Centre for Higher Education Transformation (CHET), senior researchers and the US Partnership for Higher Education in Africa to establish the Higher Education Research and Advocacy Network in Africa (HERANA).[1]

Credit must be given to the US Partnership for supporting such a complex and potentially controversial project – and one which would not easily have been funded by a single foundation. Having on board the Ford Foundation, the Carnegie Corporation of New York, the Rockefeller Foundation and the Kresge Foundation contributed to the credibility of the project amongst higher education leaders and academics. A special word of thanks must go to Dr John Butler-Adam (Ford), who 'steered' the Partnership in this project, and to Dr Claudia Frittelli (Carnegie), who participated actively throughout.

The capacity-building component of HERANA is the Higher Education Masters in Africa, run jointly between the universities of the Western Cape, Makerere and Oslo, with students from eight African countries. The Masters programme is funded by the NOMA programme of the Norwegian Agency for Development Cooperation (NORAD) with Ms Tove Kivil a constant source of support.

We must also acknowledge the vice-chancellors of the eight participating universities who expressed their confidence in the project and identified relevant staff (see Project Group below) to provide institutional data and participate in the network. The full list of project participants is included in Appendix B.

A special word of thanks must also go to Professor Manuel Castells, whose seminal 1991 paper, *The University System: Engine of development in the new world economy*, not only shifted the thinking of agencies such as the World Bank, but was an inspiration to the project group. Prof. Castells' continued participation and support is both a motivation and a challenge.

We must acknowledge the fortuitous coincidence of HERANA and *University World News* starting at almost the same time. *University World News*, with its 30 000 readers, around 14 000 of whom subscribe to the Africa edition, has been a source of information for our

---

1   For a description of the various HERANA project components, participants and publications, visit the website at http://www.chet.org.za/programmes/herana/.

project and a distribution resource. It has been a pleasure being in partnership with the editor, Karen MacGregor, who also edited the report and wrote the Executive Summary.

Finally, our thanks go to the Board of CHET, which not only expressed confidence in the CHET leadership, but participated in consultations to establish HERANA. Four members who participated actively in the project are Prof. Teboho Moja (Chair of the Board, New York University), Dr Lidia Brito (UNESCO), Dr Goolam Mohamedbhai (former Secretary-General, Association of African Universities), and Dr Esi Sutherland-Addy (University of Ghana).

The project group

Academic advisers	*Higher Education Studies*: Prof. Peter Maassen (University of Oslo) and Dr Nico Cloete (Director: CHET, and University of the Western Cape) *Development Economics*: Prof. Pundy Pillay (University of the Witwatersrand) *Sociology of Knowledge*: Prof. Johan Muller (University of Cape Town)
Researchers	Dr Nico Cloete (Director: CHET) Dr Pundy Pillay (University of the Witwatersrand) Prof. Peter Maassen (University of Oslo) Ms Tracy Bailey (CHET Project Manager) Dr Gerald Ouma (University of the Western Cape) Mr Romulo Pinheiro (University of Oslo) Dr Patricio Langa (Eduardo Mondlane University and University of the Western Cape)
Academic core data and analysis	Dr Ian Bunting (Department of Education and CHET Consultant) and Dr Charles Sheppard (Nelson Mandela Metropolitan University) collected and analysed the academic core data Mr Nelius Boshoff (Centre for Research on Science and Technology, University of Stellenbosch) collected data on research output
Project assistance	Ms Angela Mias (CHET Administrator) Ms Monique Ritter (Research Assistant) Ms Carin Favis (Transcriber) Ms Kathy Graham and Ms Marlene Titus (Funds Management)

External Commentators	Prof. Manuel Castells (University of Southern California, Los Angeles, and Internet Interdisciplinary Institute, Open University Catalonia, Barcelona)
	Prof. John Douglass (Centre for Studies in Higher Education, University of California, Berkeley)
University contacts	**Botswana**: Prof. Isaac Mazonde (Director, Research and Development), Mr David Katzke (Deputy Vice-chancellor, Finance and Administration), Mr Silas Onalenna (Assistant Director, Institutional Research)
	Dar es Salaam: Prof. Daniel Mkude (Department of Linguistics), Prof. Amandina Lihamba (Acting Director, Directorate of Public Service)
	Eduardo Mondlane: Prof. Maria da Conceição and Dr Patricio Langa (Faculty of Education)
	Ghana: Prof. Ben Ahunu (Provost, College of Agriculture and Consumer Sciences), Mr Alfred Quartey (Director, Planning), Dr Joseph Budu (Registrar)
	Makerere: Prof. Vincent Ssembatya (Director, Quality Assurance), Dr Florence Nakayiwa-Mayega (Department of Planning and Development)
	Mauritius: Prof. Kishore Baguant (Director, Quality Assurance), Prof. Henri Li kam Wah (Faculty of Science), Ms Anjana Daiboo (Office for Quality Assurance)
	Nairobi: Mr Bernard Waweru (Registrar), Mr Samuel Kiiru (Institute for Development Studies)
	Nelson Mandela Metropolitan: Prof. Heather Nel (Director, Strategic and Institutional Planning), Dr Charles Sheppard (Director, Management Information)
Network	Higher Education Research and Advocacy Network in Africa (HERANA)

Acronyms and abbreviations

CHET	Centre for Higher Education Transformation
GCI	Global Competitiveness Index
GDP	Gross domestic product
HDI	Human Development Index
HERANA	Higher Education Research and Advocacy Network in Africa
ISI	Institute for Scientific Information
NGO	Non-governmental organisation
NMMU	Nelson Mandela Metropolitan University
OECD	Organisation for Economic Co-operation and Development
PPP	Purchasing power parity
R&D	Research and development
SET	Science, engineering and technology
SME	Small and medium enterprises
UNDP	United Nations Development Programme
UNESCO	United Nations Educational, Scientific and Cultural Organisation
USD	United States Dollar
WEF	World Economic Forum

Executive summary

The context

In recent decades the phenomena of 'globalisation' and the 'knowledge economy' have been accompanied by new challenges and increasingly important roles in development for new competencies and skills as well as for research, innovation and technological development.

Higher education is now recognised as key to delivering the knowledge requirements for development. Research has suggested a strong association between higher education participation rates and levels of development, and that high levels of education are essential for the design and production of new technologies, for a country's innovative capacity and for the development of civil society.

This has persuaded many countries – including rapidly developing nations such as China and India – to put knowledge and innovation policies, and higher education, at the core of their development strategies. The ability of developing countries to absorb, use and modify technology developed mainly in high-income countries will drive more rapid transition to higher levels of development and standards of living.

The role of higher education in development in Africa has remained unresolved. Following independence, universities were expected to be key contributors to human resource needs. The idea of 'development universities' emerged during the 1970s, when it was argued that governments should steer universities towards a development role. This was not done, partly because many governments had no coherent development model, and instead steering became interference and universities became sites of contestation. States and academics became sceptical of the role of universities in development, and higher education came to be seen as a 'luxury ancillary' – nice to have, but not necessary.

During this period the World Bank, especially, concluded that development efforts in Africa should concentrate on primary education. Dramatic declines in expenditure on higher education followed: spending per student fell from USD 6 800 in 1980, to USD 1 200 in 2002, and later to just USD 981 in 33 low-income sub-Saharan African countries. Lack of investment in higher education delinked universities from development, led to development policies that had negative consequences for African nations, and caused the closure of institutions and areas of higher education that are critical to development.

During the 1990s and early 2000s some influential voices (including the World Bank) started calling for the revitalisation of African universities and for linking higher education to development. Ahead of the UNESCO World Conference on Higher Education in 2009, a group of African education ministers called for improved financing of universities and a support fund to strengthen training and research in key areas.

The research

Much research into the relationship between higher education and economic development has been econometric in nature. Little research has focused on the characteristics and dynamics of the relationship between higher education and development, or on contextual and institutional factors that facilitate or inhibit these relationships. This study addresses some of these gaps.

To understand the contributions of African universities to economic development, the report argues that the unique characteristics of universities should be a starting point. The analytical point of departure has been that the conditions under which each university contributes to economic development are influenced by the following three related factors:

- The nature of the pact between universities, political authorities and society;
- The nature, strength, size and continuity of the university's academic core; and
- The level of coordination, implementation and connectedness of universities in the larger policy context.

The aim of the project was to investigate the complex relationships between higher education and economic development in selected African countries with a focus on the context in which universities operate, the internal structure and dynamics of the universities, and the interaction between the national and institutional contexts. It also aimed to identify factors and conditions that facilitate or inhibit universities' ability to make a sustainable contribution to economic development.

The project began with a review of the international literature on the relationship between higher education and economic development. This was followed by case studies of three systems that have effectively linked their economic development and higher education policy and planning – Finland, South Korea and North Carolina state in the US.

The next phase involved collecting data at both the national and institutional levels in eight African countries and universities included in the study. In seven of the countries the national ('flagship') university was selected: the universities of Botswana, Ghana, Nairobi (Kenya), Mauritius, Eduardo Mondlane (Mozambique), Dar es Salaam (Tanzania) and Makerere (Uganda). In South Africa, the Nelson Mandela Metropolitan University (NMMU) was regarded as comparable in terms of size and profile to the other African institutions. The University of Cape Town, Africa's top-ranked institution, was included in the analysis of the academic core.

The research team visited the eight African countries and universities between February and June 2009. Interviews were conducted with a range of individuals in universities and in government ministries and agencies, and higher education commissions. The analysis also drew on policy and strategy documents at national and institutional levels, and on quantitative data including national development indicators and statistics.

A feature of the study is that concepts such as 'pact', 'academic core' and 'coordination' were operationalised by, among other things, developing and using specific indicators that allowed comparable empirical evidence to be gathered.

Evidence of a pact?

The research assumed that the stronger the 'pact' in a country (i.e. broad agreement between government, universities and core socio-economic actors about the nature of the role of universities in development), the better universities would be able to make a significant and sustainable contribution to development. From interviews and documents analysed, the most important findings in this regard were:

- None of the African countries had a clear development model or strategy, although Mauritius was moving in that direction. Some countries had national development plans (Uganda, Botswana and Mozambique), others had poverty reduction strategies (Ghana and Mozambique), and several had grand national visions cast into a distant future. But these were often based on 'best practice' policy-borrowing from first world countries, and lacked implementation plans or systematic monitoring mechanisms.
- There was lack of agreement between national and university stakeholders about a development model, except in Mauritius, and about the role of higher education in development. Mauritius came closest to a development model with a generally agreed national vision and associated policies, but coordination, implementation and monitoring was lacking. The other countries had changing national priority announcements and a range of non-complementary policies in different centres of power.
- Mauritius was also the only country that stated upfront that knowledge drives economic growth. Knowledge was not considered key to development in the other countries.
- Excluding Mauritius, knowledge economy awareness was seldom reflected in more than one ministry's policy or in national vision statements, and was mostly absent from the policies of ministries responsible for higher education. Except for Botswana and Uganda, this articulation was generally stronger at the national than at the institutional level.
- At the institutional level, the knowledge economy was articulated in the policies or plans of the universities of Botswana, Mauritius and Makerere. No university had specific policies regarding its role in economic development. But this role was embedded in the strategic plans or research policies of Botswana, Nairobi, Mauritius and Makerere.

What is the role of higher education in development? There are different notions. One, dominant in and outside universities, is an 'instrumentalist' role that assumes universities have a concentration of expertise that should be applied to pressing social problems. A second 'engine of development' notion has taken hold in many advanced countries and focuses on strengthening knowledge and innovation as crucial productive forces without which no country can participate in the global knowledge economy. A third notion is the university as 'self-governing' institution that contributes to development indirectly by, among other things, producing high-level skills and scientific knowledge. The research found that:

- At national and institutional levels, the most obvious unresolved tension was between the self-governance and instrumental roles. This reflects the well-known tension between institutional autonomy, and engagement or responsiveness.
- At national level the dominant expectation was that universities should contribute directly to development (the instrumental role), stressing contribution via expertise and capacity building rather than producing new scientific knowledge. A constant complaint was that universities were not contributing enough to development, usually referring to tackling social problems rather than economic development.
- The engine of development notion was stronger among government stakeholders than in universities, but it could be that governments see knowledge in a narrow instrumental way, rather than as an engine of development. It was surprising that support for a knowledge economy approach was weak among university leaders. The University of Mauritius was the only institution with 'engine of development' as the dominant discourse, corresponding with the view of government.

The academic core

The university's unique contribution to development is via knowledge – either transmitting knowledge to individuals (teaching), or producing and disseminating knowledge that can be applied to the problems of society and economy (research, engagement). Universities can only participate in the global knowledge economy and make a sustainable contribution to development if their 'academic core' is strong. The study investigated the strength of the academic core at the African universities, and whether the academic core was strengthening or weakening.

CHET identified eight performance indicators, some based on notions of flagship universities as producers of new knowledge and the next generation of academics, and others pertinent to the African context. The 'input' indicators were: enrolments in science, engineering and technology (SET); postgraduate enrolments; the academic staff-to-student ratio; proportion of academic staff with doctoral degrees; and research funding per academic. 'Output' indicators were: graduation rates in SET fields; and knowledge production in the form of doctoral graduates and publications in recognised ISI journals. From their scores institutions were categorised into the following groups:

- Group 1: Cape Town, the only university that was strong on all input and output ratings.
- Group 2: Mauritius, Makerere and NMMU, which had medium ratings on both the input and the output sides.
- Group 3: Dar es Salaam and Nairobi, which had overall medium ratings but which were weak on the output side.
- Group 4: Botswana, Ghana and Eduardo Mondlane, which had weak ratings on both the input and the output side.

With the exception of Cape Town, the universities were primarily undergraduate teaching institutions and did not have academic cores that lived up to expectations contained in their mission statements. Except for Cape Town and NMMU, the universities struggled to compile the data, and it became clear that an important task in developing the academic core would be to improve the definition of key performance indicators and the systematic, institution-wide capturing and processing of data.

Input indicators

There was considerable variance in the input indicators, with the strongest being manageable student–staff ratios and a relatively high level of staff with PhDs, which could partially account for solid undergraduate success rates. But success rates have to be seen in the context of a flagship university in a national system of low participation rates – their students are an elite group.

The teaching loads at all but two universities were satisfactory in 2007, and indicated that their academic staffing resources met the teaching needs of their students. The exceptions were Ghana and NMMU whose student enrolments increased at higher levels than their totals of academic staff. This finding does not support the stereotype of 'mass overcrowding' in African higher education, certainly not at flagship universities.

Two areas of great concern were low numbers of doctoral students, and lack of research funds. The dramatic increase that occurred in masters enrolments and graduations did not translate into increased enrolments in doctoral studies. In some cases, universities enrolled more than 50 masters per PhD student, when an ideal ratio should be no more than five masters per doctoral student. While coursework masters degrees increase the pool of highly-skilled workers beyond the bachelor degree – a feature of many knowledge economies – they do not seem to prepare students for doctoral studies.

Not enrolling and graduating PhDs has serious consequences. First, one of the core tasks of the flagship university in any country is to reproduce its own academic staff, and to produce academics for other higher education institutions in the system. Second, it has to respond to increasing demand in the knowledge economy for people with doctorates in institutions other than the university.

Output indicators

There was some convergence regarding output indicators, with the exception of Cape Town. Output indicator data showed varying SET graduation rates, with the highest at Botswana, Mauritius and Cape Town, closely followed by Dar es Salaam. But doctoral output was very low, with five universities producing 20 or fewer doctorates in 2007, Makerere, Nairobi and NMMU producing between 20 and 40, and only Cape Town more than 100.

In South Africa there is a high correlation between the proportion of academics with a doctorate and research publications produced at a university. 'ISI-referenced publications' represents a narrow notion of research output, but it is what makes a flagship university and its academics part of the global knowledge community.

The study showed that in 2007 more than half of permanent academics had doctorates at Nairobi, Cape Town and Dar es Salaam. This is very strong capacity. But it did not translate into research productivity. The target for permanent academics was set at one research article published every two years. Only Cape Town achieved a ratio of one article per academic per year, NMMU a ratio of one article per academic every three years, and Makerere a ratio of one every five years. At the other universities, each academic was likely to publish on average only one article every ten or more years.

During interviews with academics, three broad factors affecting the production of doctorates, research training and publication emerged.

The first was limited research funding at all the universities except Cape Town, and cumbersome procedures and restrictions on what funds can be used for, which makes consultancy more attractive. It emerged that consultancies have major advantages over research grants, providing direct supplementation of income and greater flexibility over how funds are spent, and having other benefits such as travel and being invited to join networks. But since there is no pressure to publish or to train postgraduates, consultancies do not strengthen the academic core.

Except for the South African system, the lack of incentives to publish at the African universities is also a problem, starting with very little earmarked research funding from government. Internal competitive funding sources are mostly for young academics and doctoral students, with many senior academics saying the amounts are not worth applying for. In some cases, while some money is available for equipment, it is nearly impossible to get equipment maintenance funds. Governments and universities should explore incentive systems such as that in South Africa, where the government financially rewards institutions for PhD graduates and accredited publications.

A second factor, with the exception of Cape Town, is the huge increase in taught masters courses which do not necessarily lead to doctoral study. This could be part of the serious 'pipeline' problem that is curtailing PhD numbers and, hence, an essential ingredient in the knowledge production process. The third factor distracting academics from knowledge production at these universities is supplementary teaching. Many academics teach privately within the university on 'parallel' courses for fee-paying students, as well as on courses for publicly-funded students. And many also teach outside the university in private institutions. This leaves little time or energy for PhD supervision or research and publication, weakening the academic core.

The lack of knowledge production at many of Africa's flagship institutions is not simply a lack of capacity and resources, but a complex set of capacities and contradictory rewards within a scarce-resource situation. To 'refocus' universities, attention will have to be paid to incentive structures that encourage knowledge production.

Coordination and connectedness

Knowledge policies aimed at improving the capacity of a country to participate in the global knowledge economy have become increasingly important. The study probed the coordination of knowledge policies across ministries involved with higher education, science, technology and innovation, and those responsible for economic development or planning. Regarding implementation, at the national level it looked at the role of the ministry responsible for higher education steering and funding. At the institutional level, indicators dealt with aspects such as incentives and rewards, special teaching and research programmes that link to economic development, and funding support for research.

The concept of 'connectedness' was used to depict looser forms of interaction such as the linkages and networking between the university and external groupings including business, foreign donors and community groups or agencies. The extent to which selected university development projects or centres were connected to external groups in ways that either strengthen or weaken the academic core, was also explored.

National coordination

There was a range of coordination activities in most of the African countries. Mauritius, Kenya and South Africa had the highest rating for coordinating polices and building agreement at the national level.

The most common structures for promoting coordination and consensus-building were forums. But these were said to be largely talk shops; follow-up to agreements was weak and there were few attempts to monitor progress and implement decisions. There were attempts at coordination through the creation of 'super-ministries'. A perpetual problem was the absence of cooperation between departments of education and science and technology – but merging them did not seem to guarantee more effective coordination either.

There was a lack of supporting policies across relevant departments, and the focus of policies often depended on the interests of changing government ministers. In all eight countries there were national policies that promote research and innovation, but mostly within science and technology departments. Funding from government through education departments was mainly for teaching and infrastructure, with only on average 1–3% available for research. The exception is South Africa which allocates 13% of its annual subsidy or block grant funding on the basis of the research outputs of universities. Academics often described government's contribution to research funds as 'negligible' and, in all countries, including South Africa, there was dissatisfaction with the national research councils in terms of funding and processes.

In terms of the interaction between universities and government, five of the eight countries (Mauritius, Mozambique, South Africa, Tanzania and Kenya) had some form of structure for linking universities to government, although these did not necessarily result in effective coordination. There was a strong connection between university and government leaders, but it seemed more political than productive.

In response to weak ministries, all the countries have established higher or tertiary education councils, which are more distant from ministerial influence. These structures are better placed and resourced than ministries to play a coordinating role. They are all going through some form of 'role redefinition', but for example in Botswana, Mauritius and Tanzania they are assuming a diversity of roles – from system planning to leadership capacity building and, in some, funding allocations.

Implementation

South Africa is the only country with steering capacity, a stable funding regime and a sustainable ratio of sources of income. But it does not have a vision of the role of higher education in development, so steering is mainly internal to higher education. Uganda and Mozambique have the most serious national-level capacity problems. In a number of countries the government subsidy system is unstable and discourages enterprising behaviour, 'penalising' institutions for raising third-stream income by subtracting the amounts raised from the next year's government subsidy.

At the institutional level, only the University of Mauritius had specific structures and appointments linking its activities to economic development. Most were focused on research, innovation and technology, as well as support for small and medium enterprises. Mauritius also had a focus on work-based learning, and on economic development in research and innovation clusters. NMMU also scored high on implementation. While many universities had some form of incentive for academics to engage in research, none incentivised academics to engage in (economic) development-related research or teaching per se.

Connectedness to external stakeholders

Most of the universities talked about the importance of engaging with external stakeholders in their institutional plans or research policies, and there was evidence of such engagement through teaching, research, consultancy and other forms of 'service' activities from which a wide range of external stakeholders benefited. Only two of the universities – Nairobi and Mauritius – had units dedicated to coordinating activities with external stakeholders.

Linkages with industry were generally confined to units or centres rather than at institutional-level partnerships. And except for ad hoc consultancies at NMMU and Mauritius, there was virtually no evidence of university engagement in research and development with or for industry – largely because the industrial sector in most of the countries is under-developed and there is limited private sector R&D. Some universities, such as Mauritius, are creating university-industry liaison offices.

Interaction with the private sector took two main forms. The first was in education and training, for example using people from the private sector on curriculum committees, for work placements, and for specific customised training programmes. The second, prevalent form of interaction was business development and support for small and medium enterprises.

Foreign donors

Development aid to higher education in Africa picked up in the past decade, and a CHET study estimated that about USD 1 billion was donated to higher education in Africa from 2000 to 2005. It found widely divergent approaches to development aid with no generally accepted 'development model' linking a set of key drivers for development.

Some interviewees said not all donor agencies take government priorities into account, and others spoke about tensions between responding to the agendas of foreign donors in order to secure funding, and addressing local needs. Some commented on lack of clarity about and changes in what donors want to fund. Coordination of agendas and projects was a major problem, along with the administrative effort required to account to multiple donors. There was little coordination between donors in terms of funding areas and activities.

Only two universities have established strong donor coordination structures, Dar es Salaam and Eduardo Mondlane. The latter probably received the largest proportion of donor aid among the universities, but had the weakest doctoral enrolments, partly because many doctoral candidates study overseas and, more importantly, because there was no coordinated triangle of government, university and donor support. Mozambique's government 'outsourced' research and PhD training to donors and was mainly funding undergraduate teaching.

Connecting development activities to the academic core

University leaders each identified five to ten projects or centres with an economic development or poverty reduction focus. Information was gathered on 44 such projects and centres across the universities. The initiatives ranged from long-term research programmes to short-term consultancies, institutionalised training and small business support in various fields including public health, environmental issues and poverty alleviation.

The projects fell into three groups. The first group included projects/centres that were strongly connected to national or local priorities, had more than one funding source and, in some cases, had a connection to an implementation agency. At the same time, they were strengthening the academic core through training postgraduate students, being part of international academic networks, and publishing in peer-reviewed journals and books.

A second group of projects or centres was connected to external stakeholders in some respects, and went some way towards strengthening the academic core, but were not strong on either. The third group of projects was often well-connected to external stakeholders via funding or implementation agencies, but were largely disconnected from the academic core.

Conclusion and some implications

In summary, in his seminal book *The Higher Education System* (1983), Burton Clark argued that three forces of coordination keep higher education systems from falling apart – the state, the market and the academic oligarchy. These form three nodes in a 'coordination triangle'. The study adapted Clark's triangle to depict the three nodes as government, universities and external groupings, and argues that in order for universities to sustainably contribute to development:

- There needs to be a pact about the importance of knowledge in development and the special role of the university.
- The academic core needs to be strengthened, particularly in terms of knowledge production.
- There must be greater coordination among the increasing number of actors and agencies (government departments, business and foreign donors) involved in higher education.
- University development activities must strengthen rather than weaken academic core capacity.

The following implications for African countries and universities can be derived from the findings and analysis in this report:

- It is necessary that a dialogue about the role of higher education in development be stimulated between government (and not just the education departments), higher education stakeholders and funders. Serious thought has to be given to stronger forms of policy coordination/alignment amongst the different stakeholders.
- University leadership seminars are bound to continue to disappoint as long as there is not more agreement about the role of higher education in development, and relevant government officials and key members of higher education governance structures are not part of the discussion and capacity building.
- In all the countries studied there are tertiary/higher education councils/commissions. It is important to clarify the roles and functions of these bodies, and to consider what role they can play in promoting greater agreement (pact formation) and coordination between key stakeholders around higher education and development.
- Considerably more discussion and research are required about what constitutes the academic core and how to strengthen it – just producing more postgraduates, or providing incentives for publication, will not solve the problem.
- The reward system for academics needs further study because it seems that academics are not incentivised by institutions, governments and some funders to strengthen the academic core.
- One approach to dealing with the shortage of research funds for academics that should be explored is the establishment of an Africa Research Council that could stimulate research throughout the continent on a basis of quality, and not regional or national interests.
- Concepts such as 'community service', 'third mission' and 'engagement' either tend to reflect an instrumentalist service notion of the role of higher education or have

become clichés that obscure more than clarify this role. A more useful direction might be to investigate the relationship between core knowledge activities and connectedness to external stakeholders.

- Some development-related projects/centres were world class in terms of international recognition and cutting-edge research, while also strengthening the academic core of the universities. The challenge is how to increase the number and scale of these types of activities.

- There is a need to improve and strengthen the definition of key performance indicators, as well as the systematic, institution-wide capturing and processing (institutionalisation) of key performance indicator data.

- For the university to make a sustainable contribution to development, a number of strategies need to be developed to strengthen knowledge production in higher education in Africa. Key to this will be more successful ways of coordinating and strengthening the government, university and foreign donor triangle.

Chapter 1

Introduction

1.1 Contextualising the project: The relationship between higher education and development

1.1.1 International trends

Over the past couple of decades, 'globalisation' and the emergence of the 'knowledge economy' have given rise to new economic, social, political and cultural challenges to which nations, regions and higher education systems and institutions are responding. It is widely assumed that in the context of these new challenges specific knowledge, competencies and skills – often referred to as 'human capital' – come to play an increasingly important role in developmental efforts, as do research, innovation and technological development (Castells 2002). Knowledge production, accumulation, transfer and application have become major factors in socio-economic development and are increasingly at the core of national development strategies for gaining competitive advantages in the global knowledge economy (Santiago *et al.* 2008; World Bank 1999, 2002).

Higher education institutions are seen by many as playing a key role in delivering the knowledge requirements for development. Research has, for example, suggested a strong association between higher education participation rates and levels of development. While the higher education participation rates in many high-income countries are well over 50%, in sub-Saharan Africa they are in most cases below 5% (Bloom *et al.* 2006). Furthermore, there is increasing evidence that high levels of education in general, and of higher education in particular, are essential for the design and productive use of new technologies, while they also provide the foundations for a nation's innovative capacity, and contribute more than any other social institution to the development of civil society (Carnoy *et al.* 1993; Serageldin 2000).

This type of 'evidence' has led to a number of countries putting knowledge and innovation policies, as well as higher education, at the core of their development strategies. The best known model in a developed country is that of Finland which, following the deep recession of the early 1990s, selected knowledge, information technology and education as the major cornerstones of the new (economic) development policy (Hölttä & Malkki 2000). South Korea, Singapore, Denmark, Australia and New Zealand have also followed this route successfully.

The Chinese and Indian economies have displayed unprecedented levels of sustained growth since the early 1990s. China embarked on a knowledge-based growth track by attracting massive foreign direct investment and then building indigenous knowledge capacity through huge investments in education and research. India has succeeded by making the best use of its elite education institutions and exploiting international information technology-related opportunities, in part through the deft use of knowledge assets. The Chinese and Indian economies, however, exhibit two important characteristics with respect to higher education that set them apart from both the 'East Asian tigers' of the 1980s and from some other contemporary developing countries. First, investment in higher education is seen as a parallel process (and not a consecutive one) to providing broader access to and improving the quality of primary and secondary schooling. The second, related, point illustrated in the development pattern of the Chinese and Indian economies is that the traditional growth path of domination first of primary sector activities (agriculture and mining) followed by manufacturing and then by services, does not necessarily hold.

The speed and extent to which developing countries are able to absorb, utilise and modify technology developed mainly in high-income countries, will determine whether they will be able to realise a more rapid transition to higher levels of development and standards of living. In this way, some developing countries and emerging economies have 'leap-frogged' stages of development by investing in higher education.

1.1.2   The African context

What has been the link between higher education and economic development in Africa?

The history and specifics of the African context have given rise to particular interpretations of the role of higher education in national development. Following independence, universities in Africa[2] were expected to be key contributors to the human resource needs of the countries in which they were located. There was a particular focus on the development of human resources for the civil service and the public professions. This was to address the acute shortages in these areas that were the result of the gross underdevelopment of universities under colonialism, and the departure of colonial administrators and professionals following independence.

The year 1960 was heralded in many international circles as the 'Year of Africa' and the beginning of the so-called 'development decade'. In September 1962, UNESCO hosted a conference on the Development of Higher Education in Africa. A decade later, in July 1972, the Association of African Universities held a workshop in Accra which focused on 'the role of the university in development' (Yesufu 1973). The importance of the university in newly-independent African countries was underscored by the now-famous 'Accra declaration' that all universities must be 'development universities' (ibid.). Controversially, workshop participants agreed that this was such an important task that the university could not be left to academics alone; it was also the responsibility of governments to steer universities in the development direction.[3]

---

2   At the time of independence, the higher education systems in most African countries were limited to a single national university. It is thus not possible to speak of a higher education system as such at that time.

3   Arguably, this was the last time, until 2009, that governments in Africa agreed, at least in continental statements, that universities are important for development (MacGregor 2009a).

While many nationalist African academics enthusiastically supported the role of the 'development university', seeing it as a plus in their contestations with the expatriate professoriate that dominated institutions, it sat uncomfortably with expatriates and some 'worldly' African academics. This latter group was more comfortable with the traditional model of the university as a self-governing institution (i.e. governed primarily by scholars) that predominated in the UK and the US at the time. This self-governing model was the dominant model during the first two decades following independence and there was strong agreement between universities and 'liberation' governments[4] that the role of elite universities was to produce human capital for the new state.

Despite the rhetoric about the 'development university', African governments did little to promote the development role of universities. In part this was because many of these governments had not developed a coherent development model. In addition, many had become increasingly embroiled in internal power struggles, and the external politics of the Cold War and funding agencies such as the World Bank. Instead, 'not leaving the universities alone' became interference by government, rather than steering (Moja *et al.* 1996). In turn, universities became sites of contestation – partially around the development model of the new state, and partially around lack of delivery, which included inadequate funding for the institutions. The result was that many governments, other stakeholders and academics became sceptical, if not suspicious, of the university's role in national development. This led to a notion that higher education was a 'luxury ancillary'[5] – nice to have, but not necessary – in part, because it was difficult to see what contribution universities were making to development; in part, because of prolonged economic crises and the high costs associated with higher education.

It was during this period that the World Bank, in particular, based on the infamous 'rate of return to investments in education' study (Psacharopoulos *et al.* 1986), concluded that development efforts in Africa should be refocused to concentrate on primary education. This is clearly evident in the dramatic decreases in per capita spending on higher education in Africa: 'Public expenditure per tertiary student has fallen from USD 6 800 in 1980, to USD 1 200 in 2002, and recently averaged just USD 981 in 33 low-income SSA [sub-Saharan Africa] countries' (World Bank 2009: xxvii). This is a staggering decrease of 82%.

Unlike the approach in China and India of emphasising higher education and primary and secondary education simultaneously in their development strategies, the World Bank strategy in Africa had the effect of delinking universities from development. In addition, it led to development policies that had negative consequences for African nations and their sustainable development potential. Neglect of higher education led to the disestablishment of research centres, medical schools, agricultural centres, telecommunication and technological development, business training centres, vocational schools and other areas in the higher education sector, which are critical to the development of African societies and their economies.[6]

---

4   Many of the liberation leaders had studied at foreign universities.

5   World Bank specialists suggested at a meeting with African university vice-chancellors in 1986 that higher education in Africa was a luxury; that it might be better to close some institutions, or send those needing graduate work abroad (Brock-Utne 2003: 30).

6   The decline and the commercialisation of African universities has been well documented and need not be elaborated here. See, for example, Mamdani (2008) and Fred Hayward's contribution to the US Congress Sub-committee on African Affairs (US Congress 1994).

During the 1990s and early 2000s, some influential voices started calling for the revitalisation of the African university and for linking higher education to development (Sawyerr 2004). The World Bank itself, influenced by Castells' (1991) path-breaking paper, *The University System: Engine of development in the new world economy*, started embracing the role of higher education in the knowledge economy, and for development in the developing world (World Bank 2002). This has subsequently been strengthened by World Bank-sponsored studies such as Bloom *et al.* (2006) which empirically demonstrated a relationship between investment in higher education and gross domestic product in Africa. Additional evidence has been generated by subsequent studies by the African Development Bank (Kamara & Nyende 2007) and the World Bank (2009).

Kofi Annan, then secretary general of the United Nations, strongly promoted the importance of universities for development in Africa (quoted in Bloom *et al.* 2006: 2):

> *The university must become a primary tool for Africa's development in the new century. Universities can help develop African expertise; they can enhance the analysis of African problems; strengthen domestic institutions; serve as a model environment for the practice of good governance, conflict resolution and respect for human rights, and enable African academics to play an active part in the global community of scholars.*

This rather ambitious claim for higher education was endorsed by a group of African ministers of education at a preparatory meeting for the UNESCO World Conference on Higher Education in 2009. MacGregor (2009b) reported that the ministers 'called for improved financing of universities and a support fund to strengthen training and research in key areas'.

While the above statements clearly demonstrate support for the role of higher education in development, they do little to clarify what this role is. There seem to be two different notions hidden within the idea of a 'development tool' – a direct, instrumentalist or 'service' role, and an 'engine of development' role which is based on strengthening knowledge production and the role of universities in innovation processes.

The instrumentalist role is arguably the most dominant of the two notions in Africa. For instance, the demands by, especially, foreign donors and multilateral agencies such as the United Nations and UNESCO for university revitalisation are, in many cases, underpinned by the assumption that universities are 'repositories of expertise' which should be applied to solving pressing development issues, such as poverty reduction and education for all.

This thinking of 'university as service provider' in Africa is also strongly present within academia itself, and particularly in certain post-colonial contexts. *University World News* reported that at the Association of Commonwealth Universities conference (April 2010) it was stated that: 'Universities must be "citadels not silos", defending communities around them rather than being inward-looking, if they are to actively advance global development goals' (MacGregor & Makoni 2010), and that universities must 'orientate their activities more directly towards supporting UN Millennium Development Goals' (MacGregor 2010).

The chief executive officer of the Southern African Regional Universities Association, Piyushi Kotecha, argued that in recent decades, higher education had assumed growing importance for both personal development and for driving social and economic development: 'Now more than ever before, higher education in developing nations is being expected to take on the mantle of responsibility for growth and development, where often governments fail' (ibid.).

This 'direct' instrumentalist notion assumes that universities have a concentration (surplus) of expertise, and presumably spare time, that must be applied directly, or in partnership, to pressing socio-economic issues, such as poverty, disease, governance and the competitiveness of private firms or companies.

The second role for higher education embedded in Annan's 'development tool' is Castells' 'engine of development' notion, which has become the dominant discourse for many advanced OECD (Organisation for Economic Co-operation and Development) countries. Castells (2009) described this notion as follows:

> *In the current condition of the global knowledge economy, knowledge production and technological innovation become the most important productive forces. So, without at least some level of a national research system, which is composed of universities, the private sector, public research centres and external funding, no country, even the smallest country, can really participate in the global knowledge economy.*

There have, more recently, been calls for this kind of engagement of higher education in development. For example, the high-profile African scientist at Harvard, Calestous Juma, has consistently promoted the role of higher education in science-led development through, amongst others, the UN Millennium Project Task Force on Science, Technology and Innovation (Juma & Yee-Cheong 2005). In addition, the African Ministerial Council on Science and Technology (AMCOST), established in November 2003 under the auspices of the New Partnership for Africa's Development (NEPAD) and the African Union, has created a high-level platform for developing policies and setting priorities on science, technology, research and innovation for development in Africa.

1.1.3   The focus of prior research

As Pillay's (2010a) review of the literature shows, much of the research that has been undertaken on the relationship between higher education and economic development has been econometric in nature. Examples of such studies include the following:

- Impact of higher education on economic growth, for example studies that measure the correlation between higher education participation rates (i.e. the proportion of the population with higher education qualifications) and economic growth rate or technological advance – globally, regionally or locally.
- 'Rates of return' studies which measure the private and public benefits of investing in higher education (e.g. increased tax revenues, saving and investments, or a more

productive, entrepreneurial and civic society).

- The role of higher education in producing human capital for the labour market (e.g. issues relating to scarce skills, shortage or oversupply of skills, and individual mobility).
- Studies that focus on how higher education institutions can contribute to the capabilities of private firms to take up new technologies, including the growing importance of university-industry linkages.
- The implications of the knowledge economy for higher education institutions in terms of the kinds of graduates that are required (e.g. lifelong learning, preparation for knowledge-intensive jobs etc) and the way in which research is undertaken, as well as implications for the policy and regulatory framework within which these institutions operate.

While, broadly speaking, the body of literature on higher education and economic development has grown considerably over the past couple of decades, there are still a number of limitations to the prior research conducted in this area. For instance, little work has been done which focuses on the characteristics and dynamics of the relationship between higher education and development, or to the contextual and institutional factors which facilitate or inhibit these relationships. Neither has there been much research within the African context, or that takes both national and institutional factors into account.

The current study attempts to address these gaps and to do so from theoretical perspectives offered by the fields of higher education studies, institutional theory and development economics. This implies that in developing our analytical model we did not want to follow the 'African exceptionalism' approach.[7] In our view, for understanding the contributions of African universities to (economic) development, we first and foremost have to examine these institutions as universities, taking the unique, basic characteristics of universities as a starting point (see, for example, Clark 1983). In addition, for developing a valid analytical framework we have also incorporated relevant conceptualisations from the general social sciences. As a consequence, the analytical point of departure for our model has been that the conditions under which each university in Africa, as elsewhere, is contributing to economic development are influenced by the following three inter-related factors:

- The nature of the pact between universities, political authorities and society at large;
- The nature, strength, size, quality and continuity of the university's academic core; and
- The level of coordination, effectiveness of implementation, and connectedness in the larger policy context of universities.

These, in turn, are influenced by local circumstances, for example, the nature of the economy of a country, and its political and governance traditions and culture; institutional characteristics, including the 'loosely-coupled' nature of higher education institutions; and the external relations of universities, especially with national authorities, foreign agencies and industry.

---

7   See, for example, Altbach and Balán (2007), who focused in their book *World Class Worldwide* on the transformations of research universities in Asia and Latin America. They have not included Africa because they believe 'that Africa's academic challenges are sufficiently different from those of the nations represented here that comparison would not be appropriate' (Altbach & Balán 2007: vii). Strikingly, the authors do not provide any arguments or data for their claims.

1.2   Project focus and methodology

As a point of departure, the overall aim of the project was to investigate the complex relationships between higher education (specifically universities) and economic development in selected African countries with a focus on the context in which universities operate (political and socio-economic), the internal structure and dynamics of the universities themselves, and the interaction between the national and institutional contexts. In addition, the project aimed to identify those factors (practices, strategies) and conditions (context) – at both national and institutional levels – that facilitate or inhibit universities' ability to make a sustainable contribution to economic development.

The project began with a review of the international literature on the relationship between higher education and economic development (Pillay 2010a). This was followed by case studies of three systems which have successfully linked their economic development and higher education policy and planning – Finland, South Korea and North Carolina state in the US (Pillay 2010b).

The next phase of the project involved the collection of data at both the national and institutional levels in the eight African countries and universities included in the study. These were:

- Botswana – University of Botswana
- Ghana – University of Ghana
- Kenya – University of Nairobi
- Mauritius – University of Mauritius
- Mozambique – Eduardo Mondlane University
- South Africa – Nelson Mandela Metropolitan University
- Tanzania – University of Dar es Salaam
- Uganda – Makerere University.

The countries included in the study were selected primarily on the basis of previous collaboration, and on the basis of World Economic Forum (WEF) ratings regarding location in the knowledge economy 'rankings'. The WEF's rating classifies the eight African countries and the three international case study countries according to their 'stage of development' as either factor-, efficiency- or innovation-driven. In the 'first stage of development', the economy is 'factor-driven' and countries compete based on their factor endowments: primarily unskilled labour and natural resources. As wages rise with advancing development, countries move into the 'efficiency-driven' stage of development, when they must begin to develop more efficient production processes and increase product quality. At this point competitiveness is increasingly driven by higher education and training, amongst other things. Finally, as countries move into the 'innovation-driven' stage, they compete through producing new and different goods by combining sophisticated production processes with a high-skill workforce, research and innovation. The three 'successful' systems – Finland, South Korea and the US (North Carolina) – are classified as innovation-driven; South Africa and Mauritius are classified as efficiency-driven; Botswana is moving from factor-driven to efficiency-driven; and the remaining five countries are at the factor-driven stage.

(See Appendix A for a higher education and development profile of the countries included in the study.)

In each of the collaborating countries the national ('flagship') university was selected, except in South Africa where Nelson Mandela Metropolitan University (NMMU) was regarded as a more 'comparable' institution in terms of size and profile. For the analysis of the academic core, we also included the University of Cape Town, which is the number-one-ranked university in Africa, both in the Times Higher Education World University Rankings and the Shanghai rankings.

The research team visited the eight African countries and universities between February and June 2009. Semi-structured interviews were conducted with a wide range of individuals in each country, including central actors in selected ministries and commissions/councils for higher education and other stakeholders at the national level; and in universities, institutional leadership, senior academics, administrators and project leaders. (See Appendix B for the list of interviewees.) The interviews with institutional stakeholders were transcribed, enabling direct quotation in the case study reports. Transcription of the national stakeholder interviews was not always possible as in some cases these were not recorded owing to government 'sensitivities'.

The analysis also drew on various policy and strategy documents (national and institutional levels), as well as quantitative data including national development indicators and statistics relating to the higher education systems and universities in the sample.

Throughout the project process, various efforts were made to engage with the national and institutional stakeholders in each of the eight African countries that participated in the project, in order to obtain feedback regarding the accuracy and completeness of data collection, as well as the interpretation of the data:

- During 2009 and 2010, work-in-progress was presented via seminars to stakeholders in six of the African countries, and to academics in the field such as at the Consortium of Higher Education Researchers (CHER) conference (Oslo 2010) and the University of the Western Cape seminar with Manuel Castells (Cape Town 2009).
- In the drafting of the case study reports, additional information as well as clarification was obtained from national and institutional stakeholders via email. The information gathered on the development projects was compiled in table form and emailed to the respective project leaders with a request to check for accuracy and to fill in any gaps.
- In August 2010, the draft case study reports were emailed to the vice-chancellor and one or two other institutional leaders, as well as the project leaders, in each of the eight universities to request their feedback. A two-day seminar[8] was held in South Africa that month, attended by at least two representatives from each country, during which detailed feedback was obtained on the reports.

---

8   For more information about this seminar, visit the CHET web site: http://chet.org.za/higher-education-and-economic-development-africa-report-back-herana.

A feature of this study is that core concepts such as 'pact', 'academic core' and 'coordination' were operationalised through, amongst other things, the use of specific indicators, which allowed us to gather comparable empirical evidence. Throughout the project process, team members met to discuss their ratings and interpretations of the research findings as these were emerging and to further develop the analytical framework for the study.

1.3   Analytical starting points for the study

In the knowledge economy, universities are considered to be key institutions for the production of high-level skills and knowledge of relevance for private and public sector innovation process, based on the traditional core business of universities – the production, application and dissemination of knowledge.

In many countries, higher education has become one of the central areas in the government's knowledge policies. This means that more policy/political actors than the ministry of education, as well as socio-economic stakeholders (employers' organisations, funders and research councils), have become interested in higher education and involved in higher education policy. As a consequence, system- and institutional-level coordination of knowledge policies with adequate structures and processes within the political system have become major issues, most notably the capacity to coordinate different political activities of the governing of knowledge production, reproduction and coordination.

As mentioned earlier, to get a better understanding of the relationship between higher education and development, the research group undertook case studies of systems where there is a well-established integration of higher education in national development strategies. The three case studies are Finland, South Korea and the state of North Carolina in the US – all three located in OECD member countries on different continents. One of the main reasons for choosing these three was that in all cases there was evidence of a strong and close relationship between education and economic development in general, and higher education and economic development in particular. In addition, in all three systems a rethink of major economic policies was accompanied by a deliberate attempt to link higher education to economic development.

Of particular interest to our study was the question: What is it about these three systems that enable them to successfully link higher education to economic development? Put another way: What are the core conditions that are present in each of the three systems that enable their higher education sectors to successfully and sustainably contribute to development?

Common to all three systems was a strong, agreed-upon framework for economic development aimed at realising an advanced, competitive knowledge economy, and an important role for higher education in this regard. Despite major contextual differences, the three systems exhibited the following conditions for harnessing higher education for economic development:

- Their higher education systems had been built on a foundation of equitable and quality schooling. There was also an emphasis on achieving high quality higher education.
- They had achieved very high participation rates in higher education (see Appendix A).
- Their higher education systems were differentiated (institutional and public/private) as part of achieving their human capital, research and innovation objectives for economic development.
- Their governments ensured a close link between economic and (higher) education planning.
- There were effective partnerships and networks between the state, higher education institutions and the private sector to ensure effective education and training, and to stimulate appropriate research and innovation.
- There was strong state involvement in a number of other respects including, for example, adequate state funding for higher education; using funding to steer the higher education sector to respond to labour market requirements; and incentivising research and innovation in the higher education sector.

Drawing on the review of the literature (Pillay 2010a), the implications from the case studies of three successful systems (Pillay 2010b), and preliminary observations from the eight African case studies, we formulated the following analytical propositions:

- A condition for effective university contributions to development is the existence of a broad pact between government, universities and core socio-economic actors about the nature of the role of universities in development.
- As a core knowledge institution, the university can only participate in the global knowledge economy and make a sustainable contribution to development if its academic core is quantitatively and qualitatively strong.
- For linking universities effectively to development a country needs various forms and methods of knowledge policy coordination. In addition, the connectedness between the larger policy context, universities and development is crucial.

These analytical propositions provided a three-prong focus for the analysis of the data, namely: the existence of a pact on the role of universities in economic development; the nature and the strength of the academic core of the universities; and the extent of knowledge policy coordination and the connections between key stakeholders. In the remainder of this report, we further unpack these conceptual notions and present the analysis and key findings of the data.

1.3.1   What the project is not doing

As can been seen from the outline above, this study has a considerable scope. Nevertheless, the project is not attempting to:

- Measure or evaluate the extent to which universities are contributing to development, or the impact that their activities have on development in their respective countries.
- Assess the impact or effectiveness of specific institutional policies, units or development projects.
- Review the number or nature of donor projects, or examine the overall contribution of particular external donors to university development.
- Assume or assert that the primary role for higher education is development, but rather seek to investigate the factors that either facilitate or inhibit the possible contributions that universities can make to development.

Chapter 2

Universities and economic development: Evidence of a pact?

For the purposes of this study, we use the definition of a pact provided by Gornitzka *et al.* (2007: 184):

> A 'pact' is a fairly long-term cultural commitment to and from the university, as an institution with its own foundational rules of appropriate practices, causal and normative beliefs, and resources, yet validated by the political and social system in which the university is embedded. A pact, then, is different from a contract based on continuous strategic calculation of expected value by public authorities, organised external groups, university employees, and students – all regularly monitoring and assessing the university on the basis of its usefulness for their self-interest, and acting accordingly.

The key actors of the pact are national, institutional and external stakeholders. It is assumed that the stronger the pact between universities, university leadership, national authorities and society at large, the better the universities will be able to make a significant, sustainable contribution to development.

Our interest is in exploring the extent to which there is a pact around the role for higher education in society in general and in economic development in particular in each of the eight African countries. Key to the development of such a pact is agreement or consensus that there should be a role for higher education and then about what that role should entail. In order to investigate this aspect, we have sought to address the following questions:

1. Is there a role for knowledge production and for universities in the national development plan?
2. How do the relevant national authorities and institutional stakeholders talk about and conceptualise the role of universities, and is there consensus or disjuncture?

In order to investigate these various dimensions of the pact, we collected and analysed an array of both documentary and interview data. At the national level, we consulted national vision documents as well as policies, plans and/or strategies for development, higher education, and science and technology. Interviews were conducted with a range of national stakeholders, such as representatives of the ministries responsible for higher education, finance or economic affairs, and science and technology, as well as representatives from tertiary/higher education councils/commissions. At the university level, we examined key institutional documents such as the current strategic plan and the research policy. We conducted interviews with university leaders, including the vice-chancellor and/or deputy vice-chancellors, heads of research and institutional planning, deans of faculties and directors of centres, and other senior academics.

2.1 The role of knowledge and universities in development

2.1.1 A role for knowledge and universities in national and institutional policies and plans

From the interviews and policy documents it is evident that none of the eight African countries included in the study has a clearly articulated development model or strategy. Some countries have national development plans (e.g. Uganda, Botswana and Mozambique), others have poverty reduction strategies (e.g. Ghana and Mozambique), and a number of countries have national visions – usually focused far away in time (e.g. *Tanzania Development Vision 2025*, *Botswana Vision 2016*, *Ghana Vision 2020*, *Mozambique's Agenda 2025*, *Kenya Vision 2030*). However, these do not constitute development models and are often based on 'best practice' policy-borrowing from first world countries. Mauritius comes the closest to a fully-fledged development model with its generally agreed upon national vision and associated array of policies, but as yet without the requisite coordination, implementation and monitoring powers. The other countries are characterised by frequently changing national priority announcements, often around the budget speech, and a plethora of non-complementary policies in different centres of power.

In the absence of clear development models or strategies, we had to look at a range of policies from different departments, as well as medium- and long-term plans, in order to investigate whether the knowledge economy and a role for higher education in development featured. At the national level we looked at policies not only in the ministry responsible for higher education, but also in others such as economic development/planning and science and technology.

The role of knowledge and universities in national and institutional plans were operationalised into a series of indicators which are detailed in Table C1 of Appendix C. These indicators were then rated by three of the researchers for each country and university in the study. The aggregate results of these ratings are presented in the discussion of findings below.

As can be seen from Table 1, at the national level, Kenya and Mauritius exhibited the strongest awareness of the concept of the knowledge economy and a role for higher education in development, followed by Mozambique and Tanzania. However, with the exception of Mauritius, this awareness was not reflected across policies, but was predominantly found in the science and technology policy or in the long-term national vision. Most problematic, again with the exception of Mauritius, was that the concept of the

15

CHAPTER 2 UNIVERSITIES AND ECONOMIC DEVELOPMENT: EVIDENCE OF A PACT?

knowledge economy and a role for higher education in development was mostly absent from the policies of ministries responsible for higher education. (See Box 1 for a description of the policies in Kenya and Mauritius.)

At the institutional level, we looked at the universities' strategic plans and research policies to see whether the concept of knowledge economy, and a role for the university in development, was articulated. The knowledge economy was explicitly articulated in the policies or plans of the universities of Botswana, Mauritius and Makerere (Box 1), and was absent at the University of Ghana. None of the universities had specific policies regarding the institution's role in economic development. However, this role was embedded in the strategic plan and/or research policy of the universities of Botswana, Nairobi, Mauritius and Makerere. This role was not articulated in any of the institutional documents consulted for Eduardo Mondlane, Dar es Salaam or Nelson Mandela Metropolitan University (NMMU).

TABLE 1 Role for knowledge and universities in development

Indicators	Max. score	Botswana	Ghana	Kenya	Mauritius	Moz.	SA	Tanzania	Uganda
NATIONAL LEVEL	**6**	**4**	**3**	**6**	**6**	**5**	**4**	**5**	**4**
The concept of a knowledge economy features in the national development plan	**3**	2	1	3	3	2	2	2	2
A role for higher education in development in national policies and plans	**3**	2	2	3	3	3	2	3	2
INSTITUTIONAL LEVEL	**6**	**5**	**2**	**4**	**5**	**3**	**3**	**3**	**5**
Concept of a knowledge economy features in institutional policies and plans	**3**	3	1	2	3	2	2	2	3
Institutional policies with regard to the university's role in economic development	**3**	2	1	2	2	1	1	1	2
TOTALS	**12**	**9**	**5**	**10**	**11**	**8**	**7**	**8**	**9**

BOX 1

The knowledge economy and role of higher education in national and institutional policies and plans

National policies and plans

In Mauritius, there is a very explicit role for higher education in development, as articulated in national policy documents such as the *Draft Education and Human Resources Strategy* and, importantly, the policies formulated in the document *Developing Mauritius into a Knowledge Hub and Centre of Learning*. As a result of the coordinated efforts of the Ministry of Education, Culture and Human Resources, and the Ministry of Finance and Economic Empowerment (MFEE), the country has made significant moves forward in translating the policy documents into implementation of the first steps to move the country towards a fully-fledged knowledge economy. In addition, the MFEE is playing an important role in the funding of a major science, technology and innovation project in the country.

In Kenya, the major education policy document, *Kenya Education Sector Support Programme*, and the Ministry of Higher Education, Science and Technology's plan for 2008-2012, are the key policy documents setting out the government's vision on the role of higher education and the commitment to the knowledge economy. The development planning document, *Vision 2030*, is helping to translate this vision into policy implementation, albeit at a somewhat slow pace.

University strategic plans and research policies

The University of Mauritius strategic plan (2006-2015) and the *Strategic Research and Innovation Framework* (2009-2015) place the institution in a central role in contributing to the nation's economic development and consistently reflect the narrative of the knowledge economy. They emphasise research and innovation, instilling an entrepreneurial flair amongst staff and students, and linking science and technology to industry. They also align themselves to national policies in this regard, such as the move towards developing Mauritius into a 'knowledge hub'.

The notion of the knowledge economy and the contribution of higher education in general, and of the university in particular, to the country's national development framework are strongly foregrounded and operationalised in the University of Botswana's strategic plan. Mention is made of both the production of high-level skills, and research and innovation. The plan also takes into account the changes in the economy articulated in the government's *Draft Macroeconomic Outline and Policy Framework* which highlights the need to move away from a reliance on public sector stimulus to economic growth, and from the strong dependence on the diamond mining industry, to a stronger service sector economy, stimulated increasingly by the private sector.

Makerere University's current strategic plan (2008/2009-2018/2019) ties itself closely to the institution's role in development. The formulation of the plan was guided by the question: How can Makerere University reposition itself to meet emerging development challenges in Uganda? The development of the plan took into account a range of socio-economic, political and environmental concerns. This included an overview of shifts in the Ugandan economy with specific reference to the move towards a knowledge economy and the role that Makerere can play in this regard. The plan aligns itself with a number of national policies including the *National Strategic Plan for Higher Education* and the *Uganda Poverty Eradication Action Plan*.

17

CHAPTER 2 UNIVERSITIES AND ECONOMIC DEVELOPMENT: EVIDENCE OF A PACT?

FINDINGS

- The most striking finding is the lack of clarity and agreement about a development model (except for Mauritius) and the role of higher education in development, at both national and institutional levels.
- None of the eight countries has a development model per se, although Mauritius is moving in that direction.
- Mauritius is also the only country that states upfront that knowledge drives economic growth. For the other countries, knowledge is not yet considered to be key to economic development.
- There is an emerging awareness about the importance of the knowledge economy approach in all the countries and institutions. Except for Botswana and Uganda, this articulation is generally stronger at the national than at the institutional level. In addition, with the exception of Mauritius, it is seldom reflected in more than one ministry's policy, or in national vision statements.

2.1.2   Notions about the role of knowledge and universities

How do national and institutional stakeholders conceptualise the role of higher education and the university in development? And to what extent is there consensus or disjuncture between the national and institutional levels? Our analytical framework for addressing these questions comprises four notions of the relationship between higher education (especially universities) and national development. These four notions,[9] which are elaborated upon below, emerge in the interaction between the following two sets of scenarios:

- Whether or not a role is foreseen for new knowledge in the national development strategy.
- Whether or not universities, as knowledge institutions, have a role in the national development strategy.

These two sets of scenarios, and the concomitant four notions of the role of universities, are depicted in Figure 1.

---

9   These four notions are based on ideas developed by Maassen and Cloete (2006) and Maassen and Olsen (2007).

FIGURE 1 **The four notions of the role of knowledge and universities in development**

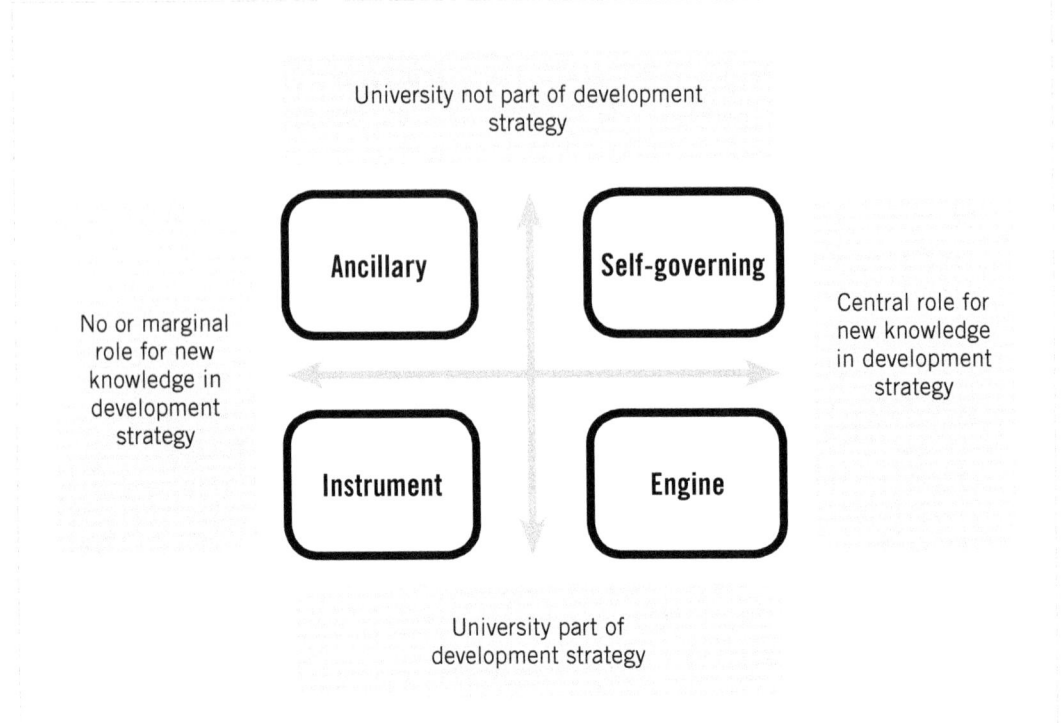

The four notions are elaborated as follows:

- **The university as ancillary**: In this notion, there is a strong focus on political/ideological starting-points for development. Consequently, it is assumed that there is no need for a strong (scientific) knowledge basis for development strategies and policies. Neither is it necessary for the university to play a direct role in development since the emphasis is on investments in basic healthcare, agricultural production and primary education. The role of universities is to produce educated civil servants and professionals (with teaching based on transmitting established knowledge rather than on research), as well as different forms of community service.

- **The university as self-governing institution**: Knowledge produced at the university is considered important for national development – especially for the improvement of healthcare and the strengthening of agricultural production. However, this notion assumes that the most relevant knowledge is produced when academics from the North and the South cooperate in externally-funded projects, rather than being steered by the state. This notion portrays the university as playing an important role in developing the national identity, and in producing high-level bureaucrats and scientific knowledge – but not directly related to national development; the university is committed to serving society as a whole rather than specific stakeholders. This notion assumes that the university is most effective when it is left to itself, and can determine its own priorities according to universal criteria, independent of the particularities of a specific geographical, national, cultural or religious context. It also assumes there is no need to invest additional public funds to increase the relevance of the university.

19

CHAPTER 2 UNIVERSITIES AND ECONOMIC DEVELOPMENT: EVIDENCE OF A PACT?

- **The university as instrument for development agendas:** In this notion, the university has an important role to play in national development – not through the production of new scientific knowledge, but through expertise exchange and capacity building. The focus of the university's development efforts should be on contributing to reducing poverty and disease, to improving agricultural production, and to supporting small business development – primarily through consultancy activities (especially for government agencies and development aid) and through direct involvement in local communities.

- **The university as engine of development:** This notion assumes that knowledge plays a central role in national development – in relation to improving healthcare and agricultural production, but also in relation to innovations in the private sector, especially in areas such as information and communication technology, biotechnology and engineering. Within this notion the university is seen as (one of) the core institutions in the national development model. The underlying assumption is that the university is the only institution in society that can provide an adequate foundation for the complexities of the emerging knowledge economy when it comes to producing the relevant skills and competencies of employees in all major sectors, as well as to the production of use-oriented knowledge.

Drawing on the information above, as well as data gathered via interviews with national and university stakeholders, we now turn to an analysis of the notions of the role of knowledge and universities in each of the eight African countries.

Table 2 captures the notions of the role of knowledge and universities of both government and university stakeholders, indicating whether the notion is strong, present, or absent for each of the categories. The table also enables us to compare government and university notions in order to assess the extent to which there is consensus or disjuncture between these two sets of actors in the pact. (See Box 2 for selected quotations reflecting the different notions of the role of higher education and the university.)

TABLE 2 **National and institutional notions of the role of the university in development**

Notions Country	Ancillary		Self-governing		Instrument		Engine	
	Government	University	Government	University	Government	University	Government	University
Botswana	·	·	□	□	■	□	□	□
Ghana	■	□	□	■	·	·	□	·
Kenya	·	·	□	■	□	■	■	□
Mauritius	·	·	□	□	■	□	■	■
Mozambique	·	·	□	■	■	□	□	·
South Africa	·	□	■	□	■	□	□	□
Tanzania	■	□	·	□	■	■	□	·
Uganda	·	·	□	■	■	■	·	□

Key:

■ Strong   □ Present   · Absent

At the national level there are three main observations. Firstly, the instrumental notion is the strongest, followed by engine of development and self-governing. Secondly, the engine of development notion is to be found mainly in science and technology policies and in national vision statements, but seldom in ministries of education – with the exceptions of Botswana and Mauritius. The references to knowledge economy, and its importance in vision statements, seem to draw considerably from 'policy-borrowing', particularly from World Bank and OECD sources and websites. Thirdly, in the case of the instrumental notion, most national government officials feel that the university is not doing enough, but there are no policies that spell out, or incentivise, this instrumental role.

Regarding the institutional notions the following observations could be made. Firstly, self-governance and the instrumental roles are the strongest positions, which reflect the traditional debates about autonomy and community engagement, respectively. This emphasis on the self-governing notion could be because the university leadership is more concerned with traditional university issues, while governments tend to be more focused on global trends. Secondly, only within the universities of Ghana and Dar es Salaam is there still a fairly traditional notion of the university producing personpower for the nation, and of the university 'knowing best what is required'. Interestingly, the leadership of neither of these two institutions expressed a knowledge economy discourse. Thirdly, Mauritius is the only institution with the engine of development as the dominant discourse, and it corresponds with the view of government. At Makerere there is considerable agreement between government and the university, except that there is an increasing awarenss at the university about the knowledge economy and the engine of development notion. Finally, at NMMU, which is an institution where a former 'traditional' university was merged with a technikon (polytechnic), all four notions are present and in contestation.

CHAPTER 2 UNIVERSITIES AND ECONOMIC DEVELOPMENT: EVIDENCE OF A PACT?

21

BOX 2

Selected narratives on the role of the university in development

I think really right from the beginning, this being the first national university, the focus had been to play a leading role in providing the necessary human capital for driving this nation. And you will see then from the Sixties, the government gave such a mandate to this university to train the critical manpower – not only to take over the positions that the foreigners were leaving, going back, but also to drive development. (University leader)

The discussion about the identity of the institution and the philosophy of education reveals a number of tensions: one body of opinion argues that the university should essentially focus on more practical, vocational training that will hopefully generate students that can find quicker employment and make a difference out there. There's another part coming from the old part of the university arguing that we should focus on more medium- and long-term development goals ... Those fault lines of debate are still very much present in the institution now. (University leader)

I think the fact that the new government separated higher education from science for me was the first sign that they really don't understand higher education. They don't understand the system. They know it's powerful, they know it's important, they know that they have to invest, but honestly I don't think they understand what higher education is all about. (Senior academic)

We firmly believe in Mauritius that knowledge drives economic growth and development. Higher education is the main source of that knowledge and of human capital. It is the knowledge promoter required for the social and economic development of any country. (National stakeholder)

FINDINGS

- In terms of notions of the role of the university in development, at both national and institutional levels, the most obvious unresolved tension is between the self-governance and instrumental roles. This reflects the well-known tension between institutional autonomy, on the one hand, and engagement or responsiveness, on the other.
- At the national level in most of the countries, the dominant expectation from higher education is an instrumental role, with a constant refrain that the university is not doing enough to contribute to development – but often referring to social problems, and not economic growth.
- The engine of development notion is stronger amongst government stakeholders than within the universities, but it could be that government sees knowledge as a narrow instrumental, rather than an engine of development notion. It is nevertheless surprising that amongst university leadership the support for a knowledge economy approach is so weak.

Chapter 3

The academic core
of eight African universities

The university's unique contribution to development is via knowledge – transmitting knowledge to individuals who will go out into the labour market and contribute to society in a variety of ways (teaching), and producing and disseminating knowledge that can lead to innovation or be applied to the problems of society and economy (research, engagement). Part of our analytical framework for understanding what impacts on a university's ability to make a sustainable contribution to development therefore focuses on the nature and strength of its knowledge activities.

According to Burton Clark (1998), when an enterprising university evolves a stronger steering core and develops an outreach structure, its heartland is still in the traditional academic departments, formed around disciplines and some interdisciplinary fields. The heartland is where traditional academic values and activities such as teaching, research and training of the next generation of academics occur. Instead of 'heartland', we use the concept 'academic core'. According to our analytical assumption, it is this core that needs to be strong and relevant if flagship universities – such as those included in this study – as key knowledge institutions, are to contribute to development.

While most universities also engage in knowledge activities in the area of community service or outreach, our contention is that the backbone or the foundation of the university's business is its academic core – that is, the basic handling of knowledge through teaching via academic degree programmes, research output, and the production of doctorates (those who, in the future, will be responsible for carrying out the core knowledge activities).

Our interest in the academic core of the eight universities in this study has the following two dimensions:

1. What is the strength of the academic cores of these universities?
2. Has there been a strengthening or weakening of these academic cores?

As mentioned, the eight African universities included in the study are Botswana, Dar es Salaam, Eduardo Mondlane, Ghana, Makerere, Mauritius, Nairobi and Nelson Mandela Metropolitan University. With the exception of NMMU, all of these institutions are considered flagship universities and are rated number one in their respective countries. These institutions are the leading knowledge-producing institutions expected to make a contribution to research and development. This is well expressed in the University of Botswana research strategy (2008: 3) as follows:

> *The university has the largest concentration of research-qualified staff and research facilities in the country and has an obligation to develop the full potential of these resources. By doing so, it can play a central part in the multiple strategies for promoting research, development and innovation that are now on the national agenda.*

NMMU was selected for the South African case study based on its comparability in terms of size and profile to the other seven institutions.

A review of the vision and mission statements of these eight universities reveals a number of common aims relating to both the nature and strength of their academic cores, as well as their contribution to development. These aims might be summarised as follows:

- To have high academic ratings, making them leading or premier universities – not only in their respective countries but also in Africa;
- To be centres of academic excellence which are engaged in high quality research and scholarship; and
- To contribute to sustainable national and regional social and economic development.

The question is: does the evidence support these ambitious aims for academic excellence? In other words, is there evidence that these universities have strong academic cores or, at the very least, are moving in that direction?

In this section, we present and discuss the findings of the analysis of data pertaining to the academic cores of the eight universities. Given that the South African university (NMMU) does not have flagship status as such, and in order to provide an 'African benchmark', we included the University of Cape Town as a ninth institution in the analysis below: Cape Town is the number one ranked university in South Africa and in Africa. We begin with a brief overview of the methodology employed in collecting and analysing the data.

3.1   Methodology

CHET started compiling data on a group of African universities in 2007 as part of a project called *Cross-National Higher Education Performance (Efficiency) Indicators.*[10] The data collected subsequent to this was discussed at a workshop in March 2009, where it emerged that although a basic data set had been compiled from institutional representatives and planners, most of the universities had experienced difficulties in completing the 2007 data templates. For a more detailed discussion on data problems encountered at the institutions, see Appendix D. Suffice to say that the first finding about the academic core is that there is a need to improve and strengthen the definition of key performance indicators, as well as the systematic, institution-wide capturing and processing (institutionalisation) of key performance indicator data.

---

10   Website: http://www.chet.org.za/programmes/indicators/.

In order to rate the strength of the academic core of the universities in the study, the following eight indicators were identified, all of which refer to characteristics or activities that reflect the production of high quality scholarship which, in turn, forms the basis of each university's potential contribution to development. The eight indicators, and the rationale for their inclusion, are outlined below. They are divided into five input and three output indicators. Some of these indicators are based on traditional notions of the role of flagship universities (e.g. the production of new knowledge and the next generation of academics) while others (e.g. science, engineering and technology enrolments and student–staff ratios) are pertinent to the African context.

Input indicators:

1. **Increased enrolments in science, engineering and technology (SET):** In African governments and foreign development agencies alike, there is a strong emphasis on SET as important drivers of development (Juma 2005). Included in SET are the agricultural sciences, architecture and urban and regional planning, computer and information science, health sciences and veterinary sciences, life sciences and physical sciences.
2. **Increased postgraduate enrolments:** The knowledge economy and universities are demanding increasing numbers of people with postgraduate qualifications.
3. **A favourable academic staff to student ratio:** The academic workload should allow for the possibility of research and PhD supervision.
4. **A high proportion of academic staff with doctoral degrees:** Research (CHET 2010) shows that there is high correlation between staff with doctorates, on the one hand, and research output and the training of PhD students, on the other.
5. **Adequate research funding per academic:** Research requires government and institutional funding and 'third-stream' funding from external sources such as industry and foreign donors.

Output indicators:

6. **High graduation rates in SET fields:** Not only is it important to increase SET enrolments, it is crucial that universities achieve high graduation rates in order to respond to the skills shortages in the African labour market in these fields.
7. **Increased knowledge production in the form of doctoral graduates:** There is a need for an increase in doctoral graduates for two reasons. Firstly, doctoral graduates form the backbone of academia and are therefore critical for the future reproduction of the academic core. Secondly, there is growing demand for people with doctoral degrees outside of academia (e.g. in research organisations and other organisations such as financial institutions).
8. **Knowledge production in the form of research publications in recognised ISI journals:** Academics need to be producing peer-reviewed research publications in order for the university to participate in the global knowledge community and to contribute to new knowledge and innovation.

We now present the summary data and ratings for the institutions included in the sample, as well as a discussion of the findings. (See Table E1 in Appendix E which shows how each of the indicators was calculated, and how the ratings were constructed.)

3.2   The academic core data

Table 3 presents the basic academic core data for the universities in the sample, indicating the changes between 2001 and 2007. Table 4 presents an overview of the ratings (or scores) per university for each of the academic core indicators. The values of the input and output indicators in Table 4 are given ratings on a scale of 1 to 3. The first three input and the three output data elements are averages for the seven-year period 2001–2007. The remaining two input indicators are based on data which were available only for 2007. Table 5 provides the average annual growth rates over the period 2001–2007.

This data set (Tables 3, 4 and 5) provides comparative data for the universities in our sample. In addition, it could be used by institutions in the eight countries as a benchmark for their own performance.

The data indicates that, apart from NMMU and Ghana, each of the universities had at least one 'strong' rating. Cape Town was rated 'strong' for all eight indicators, Mauritius for four of the eight, Dar es Salaam and Nairobi for three of the eight, and Botswana, Eduardo and Makerere for two of the eight indicators.

A large number of 'weak' ratings appear in the scores of different universities. Eduardo was rated as 'weak' on six of the eight indicators; Botswana and Ghana on five of the eight indicators. Makerere and Nairobi were rated as 'weak' on four of the eight indicators, and Mauritius on three of the eight indicators. NMMU had two 'weak' ratings and Cape Town none.

On the input side, Cape Town's overall rating was 'strong', and those of Dar es Salaam, Mauritius and Nairobi were about mid-way between 'strong' and 'medium'. Two universities, Makerere and NMMU, had overall input ratings which were close to the average 'medium' rating. Three universities – Botswana, Eduardo and Ghana – had overall input ratings mid-way between 'weak' and 'medium'. On the output side, Cape Town's average rating was 'strong', and no other university had output ratings of above 'medium', except NMMU had a 'medium' rating. The remaining seven universities had overall output ratings below the 'medium' rating.

From these scores the institutions can be broadly categorised into the following groups:

- Group 1 contains Cape Town which is the only university which was 'strong' on all input and output ratings.
- Group 2 contains Mauritius, Makerere and NMMU which had 'medium' or 'strong' ratings on both the input and the output sides.
- Group 3 contains Dar es Salaam, Nairobi and Botswana which had overall 'medium' and 'strong' ratings on the input side, but which were 'weak' on the output side.
- Group 4 contains Ghana and Eduardo Mondlane which had 'weak' ratings on both the input and the output side.

TABLE 3 Academic core indicators: Scores and changes (2001–2007)

University	% SET enrolments		Masters enrolments		Doctoral enrolments		Student–staff ratios		Student–staff ratios 2007		Doctoral graduates		Research publications		Research publication per academic	
	2001	2007	2001	2007	2001	2007	2001	2007	SET	BUS[1]	2001	2007	2001	2007	2001	2007
Cape Town	40%	42%	2 788	2 906	706	1 002	12	15	22	42	86	102	700	1 017	0.92	1.14
Botswana	22%	22%	493	951	8	41	14	27	10	59	3	4	69	106	0.10	0.14
Dar es Salaam	52%	36%	609	2 165	54	190	11	14	14	22	10	20	49	70	0.12	0.07
Eduardo Mondlane[2]	61%	48%	0	420	0	3	10	13	12	51	0	0	0	11	0.03	0.03
Ghana	22%	18%	1 344	1 580	69	102	12	31	9	68	2	20	77	61	0.12	0.08
Makerere	16%	32%	1 167	2 767	28	32	15	18	11	96	11	23	72	139	0.07	0.20
Mauritius	51%	43%	350	859	114	193	24	16	12	34	7	10	23	36	0.12	0.13
Nairobi	33%	31%	3 937	6 145	190	62	12	18	8	42	26	32	143	136	0.12	0.11
NMMU	18%	31%	1 100	1 332	175	327	31	28	26	54	27	35	154	180	0.30	0.34

Notes:

1. BUS = Business

2. 2001 figures for Eduardo Mondlane for masters and doctoral enrolments, and doctoral graduates and research publications, were not provided by the institution.

TABLE 4 Academic core indicators: Ratings per university

PERIOD >>	INPUT INDICATORS					OUTPUT INDICATORS		
INDICATOR >>	% SET enrolments	% Masters and doctoral enrolments	Student-staff ratios	% Academics with doctoral degrees	Research income / permanent academic (ppp$)	SET graduation rate	Doctoral graduates as % of permanent academics	Ratio of research publications / permanent academic
	Average for 2001–2007			2007 only		Average for 2001–2007		
RATING >>	Strong: >39% Medium: 30–39% Weak: <30%	Strong: >9% Medium: 5–9% Weak: <5%	Strong: <20 Medium: 20–30 Weak: >30	Strong: >49% Medium: 30–49% Weak: <30%	Strong: >20 000 Medium: 10 000–20 000 Weak: <10 000	Strong: >20% Medium: 17–20% Weak: <17%	Strong: >10% Medium: 5–10% Weak: <5%	Strong: >0.5 Medium: 0.25–0.5 Weak: <0.25
Cape Town	41%	19%	13	58%	47 700	21%	15.00%	0.95
Botswana	22%	5%	15	20%	2 000	20%	0.66%	0.11
Dar es Salaam	40%	9%	14	50%	6 400	19%	2.18%	0.08
Eduardo Mondlane	54%	2%	10	19%	2 000	6%	0.00%	0.03
Ghana	19%	7%	22	47%	3 400	16%	0.17%	0.11
Makerere	24%	5%	16	32%	4 900	20%	1.63%	0.09
Mauritius	48%	13%	17	45%	3 000	26%	2.80%	0.13
Nairobi	31%	16%	14	71%	5 300	14%	1.87%	0.09
NMMU	25%	6%	30	34%	12 300	15%	5.50%	0.31

Key:

▨ Strong   ▢ Medium   ▢ Weak

TABLE 5 **Academic core indicators: Average annual growth rates (2001–2007)**

University	SET enrolments	Masters enrolments	Doctoral enrolments	Doctoral graduates	Research publications
Cape Town	3.1%	0.7%	6.0%	2.9%	6.4%
Botswana	5.3%	11.6%	31.3%	4.9%	7.4%
Dar es Salaam	8.3%	23.5%	23.3%	12.2%	6.1%
Eduardo Mondlane	6.6%	n/a	n/a	n/a	n/a
Ghana	12.9%	2.7%	6.7%	46.8%	-3.8%
Makerere	16.3%	15.5%	2.3%	13.1%	11.6%
Mauritius	2.2%	16.1%	9.2%	6.1%	7.8%
Nairobi	7.6%	7.7%	-17.0%	3.5%	-0.8%
NMMU	3.7%	3.2%	11.0%	4.4%	2.6%

Note: Annual growth rates for Eduardo Mondlane are not available in the table above for masters and doctoral enrolments, and doctoral graduates and research publications, because the institution could not provide us with this information for 2001.

3.3 The strength of and changes in the academic cores

The data indicate that with the exception of Cape Town, the other universities do not have academic cores that live up to the high expectations contained in their mission statements. However, the data show considerable variance amongst the institutions in terms of input indicators, and some convergence regarding output indicators, with the exception of Cape Town.

Two input indicators with considerable variation are student-staff ratios and permanent academics with doctorates. With regard to student-staff ratios, two institutions managed to decrease the instruction loads of their academic staff (Mauritius: ratio of 24:1 in 2001 to 16:1 in 2007; NMMU: 31:1 down to 28:1) (Table 3). The student-to-academic staff ratio at Ghana increased substantially from 12:1 in 2001 to 31:1 in 2007, as did that of Botswana from 14:1 in 2001 to 27:1 in 2007 (Table 3). The ratios at other institutions increased, but not dramatically: Nairobi (12–18), Makerere (15–18), Eduardo (10–13), Dar es Salaam (11–14) and Cape Town (12–15) (Table 3).

These ratios do not support the stereotype of 'mass overcrowding' in African higher education; certainly not at the flagship universities. While one institution (Ghana) had a ratio of over 30:1, six institutions were under 20:1 (Table 3). But, these gross figures obscure substantial variations within the fields of study offered by institutions (Table 3). For example, at Nairobi, the student-staff ratio in 2007 in SET was 8:1 while it was 42:1 in business. More unfavourable examples were Ghana where the 2007 SET ratio was 9:1 and the business ratio was 68:1, and Makerere where the 2007 SET ratio was 11:1 and the business ratio 96:1. More 'normal' variations were at Cape Town which, in 2007, had a 22:1 ratio for SET and 42:1 for business, and Dar es Salaam which had 14:1 for SET and 22:1 for business.

A recent study by CHET (2010) on higher education differentiation showed that in South Africa there is a highly significant correlation of 0.82 between the proportion of the academic staff of a university that has a doctorate as their highest qualification and the research publications produced at that university. This implies that it is only in exceptional cases that academics without a doctorate publish in internationally-recognised research-reviewed journals or books.

The data in Table 4 show that in 2007 three universities had proportions of permanent academics with doctorates of 50% or higher. They were Nairobi (71%), Cape Town (58%) and Dar es Salaam (50%). This is very strong capacity – in South Africa, only three of 23 universities in 2007 had a proportion of 50% or higher of permanent academic staff with doctorates. Ghana, Makerere, Mauritius and NMMU had, in 2007, proportions of permanent academic staff with doctorates in the band 30% to 49%. Unfortunately, we do not have trend data for this indicator so we cannot comment on whether the percentages of staff with doctorates are increasing or decreasing.

The three output indicators in this study are SET graduation rates, doctoral graduates and publications in ISI-recognised journals. Starting with SET graduation rates, an average annual ratio of 25% SET graduates to SET enrolments is roughly equivalent to a cohort graduation rate of 75%, a ratio of 20% is equivalent to a cohort graduation rate of 60%, and a ratio of 15% is equivalent to a cohort graduation rate of 45%. The SET graduation rates (Table 4) show that Botswana, Makerere, Mauritius and Cape Town all have rates of at least 60% of the cohort of students graduating, while Dar es Salaam's is just under 60%. The rest are under 50%. Eduardo Mondlane, which had the highest proportion of enrolments in SET (54% of its enrolments during 2001–2007), had the poorest graduation rate.

Doctoral output is very low. Five of the universities (Botswana, Dar es Salaam, Ghana, Mauritius and Eduardo) produced 20 or fewer doctorates in 2007, while three (Makerere, Nairobi and NMMU) produced between 20 and 40, and Cape Town over 100 (Table 3). Most worrisome is that amongst all the institutions, the growth in doctoral graduations is below 10%, with the exceptions of Ghana, Dar es Salaam and Makerere, which grew from a very low base (Table 5). At the University of Nairobi, doctoral enrolments declined by 17%.

The slow growth in doctoral enrolments is in sharp contrast to the 'explosion' of masters enrolments (Table 5). At Dar es Salaam, enrolment of masters increased by 23.5% (from 609 in 2001 to 2 165 in 2007). Three other universities (Mauritius, Makerere and Botswana) had average annual increases of higher than 10% between 2001 and 2007. At the other universities growth was below 10%, with Cape Town growing less than 1% (Table 5).

As was indicated above, the fast growth in masters enrolment was not matched by a commensurate expansion in doctoral studies. For example, at Nairobi, masters enrolment between 2001 and 2007 grew at an average annual rate of 7.7% while doctoral enrolments declined. At Makerere, masters enrolments grew at an annual rate of 15.5%, while doctoral enrolments grew at only 2.3% (Table 5). The continuation rates from masters to doctoral studies seem absurdly low in certain cases. An ideal ratio of masters to doctoral enrolments should be at least 5:1, which is an indication that masters graduates flow into doctoral research programmes. In 2007, Cape Town, Mauritius and NMMU all had ratios of masters to doctoral students below 4:1. Botswana, Dar es Salaam and Ghana all had ratios between 10:1 to 23:1, while the other three – Eduardo Mondlane, Makerere and Nairobi – had ratios above 50:1.[11]

Regarding research publications, it is assumed that a flagship knowledge producer must produce research-based academic articles that can be published in internationally peer-reviewed journals and/or books. The target for permanent academics was set at one research article to be published every two years, which translates into an annual ratio of 0.50 research publications per academic. In our sample, which deals with average ratios for the period 2001–2007, only Cape Town (with an average of 0.95) met this requirement (Table 4). With the exceptions of NMMU (0.31) and Mauritius (0.13), the ratios of the other universities imply that on average each of their permanent academics is likely to publish only one research article every 10 or more years.

From the above it is evident that particularly the output variables of the universities are not strong enough to make a sustainable knowledge production contribution to development. Nevertheless, there are some positive trends in this worrisome picture. The majority of universities have strong input performance in academics with doctorates, student-staff ratios, and an increase in enrolments at the masters level. On the output side, the graduation rate of SET is quite strong for most of the institutions. There is also an increase in research output, albeit from a very low base. In 2007, Makerere produced the third highest total of research publications (139) in the sample, after Cape Town with 1 017 and NMMU with 180. Makerere showed an 11.6% growth in publication output over the seven-year period, Mauritius 7.8%, Botswana 7.4% and Dar 6.1% (Table 5). At Ghana and Nairobi, the output of ISI-accredited publications declined.

However, it should also be noted that even though the research productivity in terms of academic articles produced is increasing at the universities included, since the productivity in the rest of the world is increasing much faster, the relative position of Africa as knowledge producer is decreasing gradually. Sub-Saharan Africa contributes around 0.7% to world scientific output, and this figure has decreased over the last 15 to 20 years (French Academy of Sciences 2006).

3.4 Disjunctures between capacity and productivity

There is a long-held commonsense view that the lack of research output in African universities is simply a lack of capacity and resources. However, a closer inspection of the input-output indicators raises some interesting questions about this assumption. In order to explore this further, we selected Cape Town from group 1, Dar es Salaam from group 3 and Ghana from group 4 as representatives of these groups and plotted a comparative graph based on standardised scores (Figure 2).

---

11   These masters-to-doctoral enrolment and graduation ratios are contained in the individual case study reports for the respective universities.

The data shows that there are surprising similarities between Dar es Salaam and Cape Town in terms of input indicators such as SET enrolments (Cape Town 41%, Dar es Salaam 40%), student-staff ratio (Cape Town 13:1, Dar es Salaam 14:1) and academics with PhDs (Cape Town 58%, Dar es Salaam 50%). Ghana, on the other hand, is only similar to the other two in terms of staff qualifications. On the input side, the big difference between Cape Town, on the one hand, and Dar es Salaam and Ghana on the other, is in percentage of postgraduate students (Cape Town 19% versus Dar es Salaam 9% and Ghana 7%) and research income per permanent staff member (Cape Town USD 47 700 versus Dar es Salaam USD 6 400 and Ghana USD 3 400).

FIGURE 2 Academic core indicators (standardised data): Three selected universities

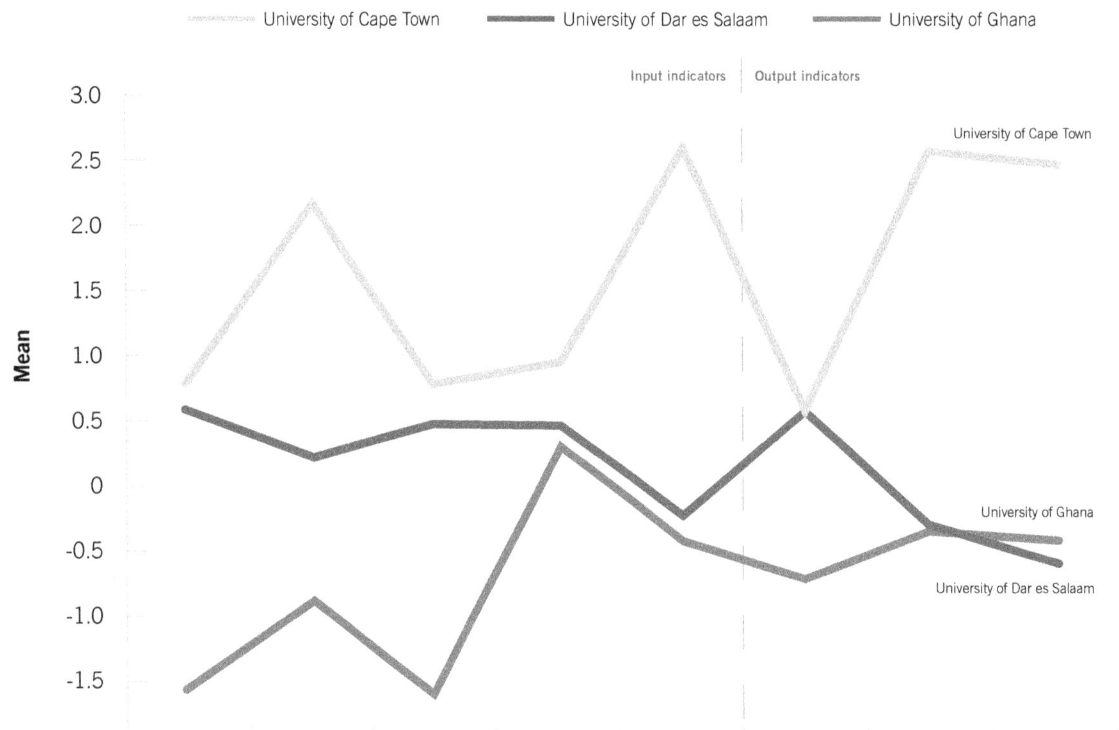

University	% SET majors	% Masters + doctorates	Student–staff ratio*	% Academics with doctorates	Research income per permanent academic ppp$	SET graduation rate	Doctoral graduates as % of permanent academics	Research publications per academic
Cape Town	41%	19%	13	58%	47 700	21%	15.00%	0.95
Dar es Salaam	40%	9%	14	50%	6 400	19%	2.18%	0.08
Ghana	19%	7%	22	47%	3 400	16%	0.17%	0.11

* In the data table the student-staff ratio is given, whilst the inverse of the student–staff ratio has been used in the graph representing the results of the k-means clustering. This was done because a high student–staff value is unfavourable and should thus reflect a low value in the k-means clustering. The University of Ghana has a high value for student–staff value in the table but the inverse shows a low value in the graph of the means for the clustering.

With regard to output indicators, Cape Town and Dar es Salaam have similar SET graduation rates (21% and 19%, respectively). The dramatic difference is in doctoral graduates (average for 2001–2007): Cape Town 15% of academic staff, and Dar es Salaam and Ghana less than 3% per academic staff member (Figure 2), and ISI publications (2007): Cape Town 1 017, Ghana 61 and Dar es Salaam 70 (Table 3).

This data poses some intriguing issues for higher education in Africa. Cape Town and Dar es Salaam have remarkably similar profiles in terms of SET (input and output), student–staff ratios and staff with doctorates, but are incomparable regarding the production of doctorates and publications. What distinguishes Cape Town from the other institutions is much higher proportions of postgraduates, research income and knowledge production outputs.

In terms of input capacity, Cape Town and Dar es Salaam are surprisingly similar, with the exception of research income (resources). Does that mean that research income is the only factor that prevents Dar es Salaam from achieving the same level of outputs as Cape Town?

During interviews with senior academics, three factors emerged that raise questions and warrant further research. The first is the problem of research funding. Not only is there very limited research funding, but the cumbersome application procedures and the restrictions on what the research funds can be used for makes consultancy money much more attractive; in other words, consultancy money directly supplements academics' income, and the researchers also have much more discretion about how it is used. The negative side of consultancy funds is that there is no pressure or expectation to publish, nor to train postgraduate students. It thus affects negatively both aspects of knowledge production, that is, postgraduate training and publishing.

Incentives to publish, as is the case in many countries, are a problem. After obtaining the professorship, publishing in international journals is not directly rewarded, but is rather a matter of prestige or 'institutional culture'. In order to incentivise this activity, universities in Africa might have to start exploring incentive systems. In South Africa, the national government subsidises each institution to the tune of about USD 45 000 per PhD graduate and USD 15 000 per accredited publication. But this is not simple correlation. Two of the universities with the highest publication rates per permanent academic (Cape Town and Rhodes) do not pass a portion of the subsidy directly to the academic or the department, but put it in a pool where everybody can compete for it.

Another dimension that certainly warrants further exploration is the relationship between research and consultancy. A PhD study by Langa (2010) suggests that having a strong academic network link, with publications, is an entry for getting consultancies. So it is not that academics choose research or consultancy; some do a balancing act between research and consultancy, while others seem to 'drift off' into consultancy and foreign aid networks.

A second problem that is affecting the production of doctorates, and associated research training and publication, is the huge increase in taught masters courses which do not lead to doctoral study. For example, the University of Cape Town had 2 906 masters enrolments and 1 002 doctoral enrolments in 2007. In contrast, in 2007 Dar es Salaam had 2 165 masters students and only 190 doctoral enrolments (Table 3). This means that there is a serious 'pipeline' problem at universities like Dar es Salaam. This could be because the masters degree does not inspire sufficient confidence in students to enrol for the PhD, or because there are no incentives to do so, or because individuals are pursuing their PhD degrees abroad. Whatever the reason, the effect is a serious curtailing of PhD numbers and hence of an essential ingredient in the knowledge production process.

According to the discussions with interview respondents, the third factor that distracts academics from knowledge production is supplementary teaching. On the one hand, the new method of raising third-stream income – namely, the innovation of private and public students in the same institution, with additional remuneration for teaching the private students – has the result that within the university, academics are teaching more to supplement their incomes. On the other hand, the proliferation of private higher education institutions, some literally within walking distance of public institutions, means that large numbers of senior academics are 'triple teaching'.

PhD supervision, in a context where the candidate in all likelihood does not have funds for full-time study and where there are no extrinsic (only intrinsic) institutional rewards, is a poor competitor for the time of the triple-teaching academic. The same applies to rigorous research required for international peer-reviewed publication: it is much easier and far more rewarding to triple teach and do consultancies.

The implication of the above is that the lack of knowledge production at Africa's flagship universities is not a simple lack of capacity and resources, but a complex set of capacities and contradictory rewards within a scarce-resource situation. This results in a fundamental lack of a strong output-oriented research culture at these universities.

FINDINGS

- The knowledge production output variables of the academic cores are not strong enough to enable universities to make a sustainable contribution to development.
- None of the universities in the HERANA group seem to be moving significantly from their traditional undergraduate teaching role to a strong academic core that can contribute to new knowledge production and, by implication, to development.
- Amongst the universities there is considerable diversity regarding input variables. The weakest indicators are the low proportion of postgraduate enrolments and the inadequate research funds for permanent staff, with the strongest input indicators in manageable student-staff ratios and well-qualified staff.
- On the output side, SET graduation rates are generally positive. But there is a convergence around low knowledge production, particularly doctoral graduation rates and ISI-cited publications.
- The most serious challenges to strengthening the academic core seems to be the lack of research funds and low knowledge production (PhD graduates and peer-reviewed publications).
- The low knowledge production cannot be blamed solely on low capacity and resources; the problematic incentive structure at these universities require further study.
- There is a clearly identified need to improve and strengthen the definition of key performance indicators, as well as the systematic, institution-wide capturing and processing (institutionalisation) of key performance indicator data.

We continue to explore some of these and other issues relating to the strength or otherwise of the academic core in the next section, where we undertake an analysis of a selection of development-related projects and their relationship to the academic core of the eight universities in the broader study.

Chapter 4
Coordination and connectedness

As highlighted in section 1.3, our analytical framework proposes that the following three interrelated factors need to be in place in order for universities to make a sustainable contribution to development: agreement amongst the major actors (pact) about the role of universities in development; academic core capacity in universities; and coordination of and connectedness between the policies and activities of government, universities and external groupings.

In this section we focus on the latter aspects of coordination and connectedness. In this project 'coordination' is used to refer to more structured forms of interaction, mainly between government and institutions; in other words, the knowledge policies and implementation activities of different government departments, particularly departments of education, science and technology, and research councils.

Knowledge policies have become increasingly important in the context of the knowledge economy. Broadly speaking, knowledge policies refer to political mechanisms (such as policies and incentives) that are aimed at improving the (knowledge) capacity of a country to participate in the global knowledge economy. Such policies thus relate to the higher education and science and technology sectors, and to high-level skills training, research and innovation. The coordination of knowledge policies can take place at the level of both policy formulation and policy implementation. Braun (2008) distinguishes between 'negative' and 'positive' coordination. He defines negative coordination as follows (Braun 2008: 230):

> ... [where] actors – for example, two ministries – are not completely independent in their decision-making but obliged to take into account a negative backlash against their own actions by the other actor. ... Negative coordination is a non-cooperative game that leads ... to the mutual adjustment of actors, but not to concerted action nor to cohesiveness of policies.

Positive coordination goes beyond mutual adjustment: 'Instead, actors start to cooperate with each other in order to deliver certain services ... It typically develops at the ministerial or agency level' (ibid.). Positive coordination is a necessary but not sufficient condition for effective policy coordination. What is required is 'policy integration' (the coordination of goals) and 'strategic coordination' ('the development of encompassing common visions and strategies for the future') (ibid.: 230–231). These last two types of coordination point to the need for consensus or a pact. As Braun (ibid.: 230) observes: 'Policy coordination as such does not absolutely need a whole-government perspective, but it implies at a minimum a perspective that is agreed upon by a number of political actors.'

Of specific interest to this study is the coordination of knowledge policies across ministries involved with higher education, science, technology and innovation, as well as those responsible for economic development or planning.

Implementation can be regarded as a component of the coordination of government policies and is a complex combination of agreement (relevant parties support the policy) and capacity to design and apply the implementation mechanisms or instruments. At the national level we looked at the role of the ministry responsible for higher education, steering and funding. At the institutional level, indicators were used that dealt with aspects such as units or structures to implement strategic plans, incentives and rewards, special teaching and research programmes that link to economic development and funding support for research.

We use the concept of 'connectedness' to depict looser forms of interaction such as the linkages and networking between the university and external groupings including business, foreign donors and community groups or agencies. We also explore the extent to which 44 development projects or centres identified by institutional leadership are connected to external groupings in ways that either strengthen or weaken the academic core of the universities.

In this section, we address the following three questions:

1. Do governments coordinate policies and programmes that are aimed at enabling the universities to contribute to development?
2. Do the universities connect to external groupings in ways that promote development?
3. Do development activities in the universities strengthen or weaken their academic core?

4.1   Coordination and implementation of knowledge policies

4.1.1   National coordination

In this section, we present and discuss findings regarding the extent to which there is coordination of knowledge policies and activities at the national level. Table 6 summarises the ratings of the coordination indicators for the eight African countries and universities in the study (see Table C2 in Appendix C for an elaboration of these indicators). As can be seen, Mauritius rates the highest at both national and institutional levels.

The two countries that scored highest on knowledge policies – Mauritius and Kenya (Table 1, section 2.1.1) – also have the highest rating for coordinating policies and building agreement at the national level (Table 6 and Box 3). To this list is added South Africa. The most common structure for promoting coordination and consensus-building were forums. However, feedback from interviewees suggested that these are seldom more than talk shops; follow-up to agreements is weak and there are few attempts at monitoring progress and the implementation of decisions. Even in countries such as South Africa, where there are stronger forms of coordination such as ministerial clusters, the same lack of follow-through occurs. In other cases, the efficacy of the structure is undermined by different departments sending officials of different ranks to meetings, leading to a gradual loss of confidence in the structure. The exception is Mauritius, where considerable effort is being made with multiple structures and networks to broaden agreement and buy-in.

TABLE 6 **Coordination of knowledge policies**

Indicators	Max. score	Botswana	Ghana	Kenya	Mauritius	Moz.	SA	Tanzania	Uganda
NATIONAL LEVEL	9	3	3	6	7	4	6	4	3
Economic development and higher education planning are linked	3	1	1	2	3	1	2	1	1
Coordination and consensus building of government agencies involved in higher education	3	1	1	2	2	1	2	1	1
Link between universities and national authorities	3	1	1	2	2	2	2	2	1

There was also evidence of attempts at coordination through the creation of 'super-ministries'. For instance in Mauritius, in order to implement plans to turn the country into a knowledge hub, a Ministry of Education and Scientific Research was created. This was then reorganised into the Ministry of Education, Culture and Human Resources and, in May 2010, reorganised once again into the Ministry of Tertiary Education, Science, Research and Technology. Kenya also established a Ministry of Higher Education, Science and Technology in 2008 (although, according to one interviewee, this had more to do with coalition politics than it did with attempts at policy coordination). Mozambique, in line with a very advanced Science, Technology and Innovation policy, established a Ministry of Higher Education, Science and Technology in 2000 but, in 2009, dissolved it into separate ministries of Education, and Science and Technology. South Africa, having a very sophisticated policy in the Department of Science and Technology, but not in Education, recently established a Ministry of Higher Education and Training, keeping a clear separation between science and higher education. A perpetual problem in the countries investigated, and in many international systems, is the absence of cooperation (Braun's 'negative coordination') between departments of education and science and technology – but merging them does not seem to guarantee positive policy coordination either.

In terms of the interaction between universities and government, in all three of the 'successful' systems (Pillay 2010b), networks play an important 'connecting' role. In North Carolina the networks seem stronger than the structures, while in South Korea there are both formal structures coordinated under the prime minister's office, and networks of academics and business leaders who had studied at particular universities such as the University of Seoul and abroad – mainly in the US. These networks are both political and productive, meaning they also foster collaboration on projects and new initiatives.

Five of the eight African countries in the study (Mauritius, Mozambique, South Africa, Tanzania and Kenya) had some form of structure or platform for linking universities to government, although these did not necessarily result in effective coordination (Box 3). What we observed in our sample of African countries is a strong connection between university and government leadership, although it seems more orientated towards the political than to the productive. It could be argued that the two are actually too close, because we encountered the constant refrain of policy instability, meaning that when there is a political leadership change in government, it affects both government departments and the university. Policy reversals, and associated staff changes described above in Mozambique, is an exacerbated example.

In response to weak ministries, and in following international best practices, all the countries in the sample have established higher or tertiary education councils, which are with few exceptions better resourced than the national ministries – and are more distant from direct ministerial influence. These structures are better placed and resourced than traditional ministries to play a coordinating role. However, these relatively new institutions are all going through some form of 'role redefinition'; most were started as quality/ certification bodies, but as is the case, for example, in Botswana, Mauritius and Tanzania, they are increasingly assuming a diversity of roles – from system planning to leadership capacity building and in, some cases, even making funding allocations.

BOX 3

COORDINATION OF KNOWLEDGE POLICIES AND ACTIVITIES

Linking economic and higher education planning

In none of the eight African countries is there an explicit link between economic and higher education planning. In Mauritius, the history of economic development over the past two decades suggests the existence of informal structures that ensure a high degree of linkage between economic and education planning. The close cooperation between the Ministry of Education, Culture and Human Resources and the Ministry of Finance and Economic Empowerment is testimony to this.

In South Africa, the institutional structures for the coordination of economic and education policy exist in, for example, the Presidency's Policy Unit and, recently, in the National Planning Commission that was established in late 2009. Policy documents such as the *Human Resource Development Strategy for South Africa*, the *Accelerated and Shared Growth Initiative for South Africa* and *Industrial Policy Action Plan* have also taken up the need for coordination between the two sectors. Moreover, the higher education institutional funding policy provides incentives for institutions to produce more PhDs and rewards peer-reviewed publications.

In Kenya there is evidence of a degree of cooperation on this between the Ministry of Higher Education, Science and Technology and the President's Office, which is responsible for the design and implementation of the country's major policy document, namely *Kenya Vision 2030*. However, there is little evidence of explicit economic and education planning. >>

BOX 3 continued ...

Coordination and consensus-building of government agencies in higher education

In Mauritius, there is evidence of consensus-building in higher education between the Ministry of Tertiary Education, Science, Research and Technology, the Tertiary Education Commission and higher education institutions. However, this appears to be intermittent and taking place in the absence of specific forums for this purpose. In South Africa a specific forum, Higher Education South Africa, has been established for coordination and consensus-building between the Department of Higher Education and Training and universities. Former President Mbeki also created a Higher Education Working Group primarily to assess the role that universities can play in the country's development. In Kenya, there is some evidence of informal collaboration between government, universities and donors on higher education goals and implementation.

Structures linking universities and governments: The national commissions

All of the eight countries have regulatory bodies (called councils or commissions of higher or tertiary education) that constitute the link between higher education institutions and the government. However, the effectiveness of these institutions varies in terms of their regulatory and other functions. In Mozambique and Tanzania, it is not possible, on the basis of available information, to comment on the effectiveness of their regulatory bodies, namely the National Council for Higher Education and the Commission for Universities, respectively. In Uganda, the National Council for Higher Education appears to be regulating public universities and undertaking appropriate research. In Mauritius and Botswana, the Councils appear to be relatively influential in policy-making and regulation. In both Ghana and Mauritius, they play a prominent role in institutional funding. In Kenya, the commission appears to be relatively weak in relation to its role and responsibilities vis-à-vis public universities, but appears to be playing a much more appropriate role with respect to private universities. In South Africa, the Council on Higher Education is supposed to play both an advisory policy role to the ministry and act as a qualification regulator. In practice, however, it is the latter role in which it has been most active up to now.

FINDINGS

- At the national level, there are considerable coordination activities in most countries, ranging from forums to clusters and the reorganisation of national ministries. However, this is mostly weak or 'symbolic' coordination.
- There are certainly many tight networks between government officials and university leadership, but it seems these are more orientated towards political connections.
- In all the countries, tertiary or higher education councils have been established, partially to compensate for weak ministries, and also to do 'independent' certification and quality assessments. Currently they are all undergoing 'role redefinitions', but could become key players in coordination and implementation monitoring.

4.1.2   Implementation

Table 7 summarises the ratings of the implementation indicators for the eight countries and universities (see Table C2 in Appendix C for an elaboration of these indicators).

TABLE 7 Implementation of knowledge policies and activities

Indicators	Max. score	Botswana	Ghana	Kenya	Mauritius	Moz.	SA	Tanzania	Uganda
NATIONAL LEVEL	12	8	8	8	8	5	11	7	6
Role of the ministry responsible for higher education	3	2	2	2	2	1	2	2	1
Implementation to 'steer' higher education towards development	3	2	1	1	2	1	3	2	1
Balance/ratio of sources of income for institutions	3	2	3	3	2	1	3	1	2
Funding consistency	3	2	2	2	2	2	3	2	2
INSTITUTIONAL LEVEL	18	10	8	8	13	7	13	10	10
Specific units, funding or appointments linked economic development	3	1	1	1	3	1	1	1	1
Incentives and rewards for development-related activities	3	2	1	2	1	2	2	1	2
Teaching programmes linked to the labour market	3	3	2	1	2	1	3	2	2
Special programmes linking students to economic development	3	1	1	2	3	1	2	3	1
Research activities are becoming more economy-oriented	3	2	2	1	3	1	2	2	3
Levels of government and institutional funding for research	3	1	1	1	1	1	3	1	1
TOTALS	30	18	16	16	21	12	24	17	16

South Africa is the only country with steering capacity, a stable funding regime and a sustainable ratio of sources of income. However, it does not have a vision of the role of higher education in development, meaning that steering is mainly based on dealing with issues internal to the higher education system. The two systems that appear to have the most serious national-level capacity problems are Uganda and Mozambique, with the latter being de-capacitated by the dissolution of the Ministry of Higher Education, Science and Technology.

In a number of countries the government subsidy system is not only unstable, it also discourages enterprising behaviour through a system that 'penalises' institutions for raising third-stream income by subtracting the amounts raised from the next year's government subsidy.

BOX 4

IMPLEMENTATION OF KNOWLEDGE POLICIES AND ACTIVITIES

South Africa rates 'strong' on three implementation indicators: Implementation to 'steer' higher education towards development; balance/ratio of sources of income for institutions; and funding consistency. South Africa uses the institutional funding formula to steer the system by providing incentives for doctoral study and publications. The university funding system is diversified between government provision, tuition fees, and institutional own income. Finally, the country provides a good practice model of consistency in funding based on higher education institutional plans, government budget constraints, and the medium term expenditure framework.

Ghana and Kenya rate high on the indicator 'balance/ratio of sources of income for institutions'. In the case of Ghana, there is evidence of attempts at both funding innovation and diversification of institutional funding sources. In the case of the former, a percentage of value-added tax is used to fund higher education capital expenditure, student loans and research. With regard to the latter, student fees are rising relative to government funding. Kenya (as well as Uganda) has developed a dual-track tuition-fee scheme to address the challenge of declining state funding. The scheme, which is highly inequitable, provides free education for a specific number of students who produce the best results in the school-leaving examinations, and charges fees to everybody else who is admitted. The inequity stems partly from the fact that most of those who get the full scholarships also attended the best schools in the country, and most often come from the richest households.

Implementation at the institutional level, refers to units or structures linked to economic development, incentives for such activities, funding available, special programmes linked to the labour market and research activities that are economy-orientated (Box 5).

Of the eight universities in the sample, the University of Mauritius is the only one with a number of specific structures and appointments linking the institution's activities to economic development. Most of these are focused on research, innovation and technology, as well as support for small and medium enterprises (SMEs). Mauritius also has a well-established focus on work-based learning, and a strong focus on economic development in its research and innovation clusters.

Interestingly, although NMMU has a low knowledge economy score (Table 1), it scores high on the implementation ratings. The university has set targets for enrolments in fields considered to be of high economic relevance and, of all the eight universities, has the highest level of research funding from both government and the institution. There are also moves towards the introduction of special programmes linking students to the labour market, and towards introducing an economic development focus into research agendas.

In the other universities, evidence of structures, appointments or funding for activities linked to economic development was only to be found in specific pockets in the institution.

While many of the universities had some form of incentive for academics to engage in research (e.g. Makerere), none of the universities incentivised their academic staff to engage in (economic) development-related research or teaching per se. At NMMU, there are (financial) incentives for academics to get involved in innovation but there are no incentives to get involved in other forms of engagement activities (e.g. community service or outreach), in terms of funding or time allocation. There are plans to develop a policy on the recognition and reward of research, teaching and engagement activities as well as the development of a workload policy that will ensure an appropriate balance between teaching, research and community engagement responsibilities.

BOX 5

IMPLEMENTATION OF KNOWLEDGE POLICIES AT INSTITUTIONAL LEVEL

Specific units, funding or appointments linked to economic development

Over the years, the University of Mauritius has established a number of appointments and structures linked to furthering the institution's activities in relation to economic development:

- The Office of the Pro Vice-Chancellor for Research, Consultancy and Innovation, which manages and provides facilities and funding for all research, innovation and consultancy activities in the institution.

- The Consultancy and Contract Research Centre which coordinates all consultancy and contract research between the university and government, industry and other stakeholders.

- The Technology Management Group, which liaises between the university and external companies around research collaboration and the commercialisation of results.

- The Excellence Park with Multidisciplinary Centres of Excellence, the aim of which is to address national priorities and opportunities through promoting research and development.

- The University Support Network for Small and Medium Enterprises, which aims to utilise university resources to contribute to the development and enhancement of SMEs, in line with the government's policy for promoting the sector.

Special programmes linking students to economic development

In recent years there has been increased emphasis at the University of Dar es Salaam on entrepreneurial training and small business development, in response to changes in the economy and wider business environment. The university has a policy on entrepreneurship which requires that every student is exposed to entrepreneurship training. While some faculties and colleges offer a separate entrepreneurship course, others have mainstreamed entrepreneurship into their programmes. A Postgraduate Diploma and a Masters programme in Entrepreneurship and Enterprise Development have also been introduced.

In partnership with the University of Bradford, the University of Mauritius was awarded a grant from the England-Africa Partnerships in Higher Education project of the British Council to incorporate work-based learning into the undergraduate curricula and to support work placements for undergraduate students to improve their employability. The Work-Based Learning Unit identifies and trains mentors from industry who provide guidance and support to students during their work placements. These mentors also assess the students on a range of competencies including communication, team work, improving own learning and performance, solving problems, working and applying numbers, using information technology and developing professionalism. >>

Box 5 continued...

Teaching programmes linked to the labour market

In 2006, the national Department of Education in South Africa required NMMU to identify five academic growth areas as part of its Institutional Operational Plan and enrolment plan for the period 2006-2010. The university consulted a wide range of national policy documents and economic growth strategies in order to identify the five priority areas which included: infrastructure development; environmental and natural resource management; economic and business development; community and health development; and education, culture and communication.

The University of Botswana's strategic plan highlights specific targets for undergraduate enrolments at the discipline level (following the *Student Enrolment Projections to 2016* report, published in 2008). The targets for 2016 include Business and Information and Communication Technology 20%; Science, Engineering and Health Sciences 30%; Humanities and Social Sciences 31%; and Education 19%.

Research activities are becoming more economy-oriented

The University of Botswana has identified a number of priority research themes based on existing areas of research strength, national research priorities, international research trends, and emerging social needs. This institutional research agenda includes a direct economic development focus in the economic diversification and entrepreneurship theme, as well as an indirect focus in other themes linked to sustainable development and poverty reduction.

Makerere University has an institutional research agenda which is driven by the university and its researchers, by national priorities and, at times, by the agendas of foreign donors. The current, multidisciplinary research agenda is informed by the government's *Poverty Eradication Action Plan*. An economic development focus is inherent, albeit indirectly, in most of the themes, such as: education for development; food and nutrition; sustainable environment development; natural resources utilisation and conservation; and cross-cutting themes such as appropriate technology, economics and biotechnology.

The University of Mauritius' *Strategic Research and Innovation Framework* outlines a number of priority clusters for research and innovation activities. A number of these include an economic development focus, such as those relating to science and technology and to transforming the Mauritian economy, while others have an indirect focus as they relate to health and the environment.

FINDINGS

- At the national level one of the weakest aspects of linking higher education to economic development is implementation: most ministries of education do not have steering instruments or mechanisms.
- Some ministries disincentivise institutions from generating third-stream income.
- Every university has at least one development-related structure and one or more special programme/s. The problem is that in too many cases these initiatives are driven by individuals rather than being institutionalised. In addition, these special implementation efforts need to be more connected.
- Despite policies that extol the importance of research related to development activities (mainly through focus themes), few institutions have special funds for this. Neither is research related to development rewarded through incentives beyond the traditional academic promotion system.

4.2   University connectedness to external stakeholders

4.2.1   Industry and community

Most of the universities in the sample talk about the importance of engaging with external stakeholders in their institutional plans or research policies. Indeed, in all of the universities there was evidence of such engagement through their teaching, research, consultancy and other forms of 'service' activities. A review of a selection of development-related activities in the eight universities (see section 4.3) indicates that a wide range of external stakeholders stand to benefit from the teaching, research and service undertaken by academics – from government, foreign donors, industry, the private sector and non-governmental organisations (NGOs) to fishers, small-scale farmers, street traders and people living with disease burdens. Universities also collaborate with or undertake work on behalf of a range of external stakeholders, especially government, industry, the private sector, and non-governmental or community-based organisations.

While these linkages were not a key focus of this study, we did gather some evidence on the nature and extent of the universities' interactions with the key external stakeholders during the interviews – in particular with industry and the private sector (including SMEs), and foreign donors (section 4.2.2).

While there was evidence of linkages with industry and the private sector in all eight universities, this was generally confined to the level of units or centres rather than institutional level partnerships or linkages. In addition, except for ad hoc consultancies at NMMU and Mauritius, there was virtually no evidence of university engagement in research and development (R&D) with or for industry. To a large extent this is because the industrial sector in most of these countries is under-developed, and because there is very limited private sector R&D – where global companies do have operations in African countries, their R&D is usually undertaken elsewhere. Of course, this is a problem in most developing countries but it is particularly acute in Africa. Some of the universities are beginning to address the lack of interaction between their institutions and industry or the private sector through the establishment of university-industry liaison offices (e.g. Mauritius). Some interviewees suggested that part of the problem is also the attitudes of academics, some of whom are unwilling to engage with external stakeholders.

Evidence of interaction with the private sector took two forms. The first is in the area of education and training. Examples include the use of people from the private sector on advisory committees responsible for curricula design and revision (Mauritius and Botswana); work placements; and for specific, customised training programmes. The second and most prevalent form of interaction is business development and support for SMEs. Examples include: the business incubator projects or units at Mauritius and Dar es Salaam; the Automotive Components Technology Station at NMMU; the Innovation Systems and Clusters Programme in Eastern Africa operating at Eduardo Mondlane, Dar es Salaam and Makerere; the Uganda Gatsby Trust at Makerere; the University of Botswana Business Clinic; and, the African Clothing and Footwear Research Network at Nairobi.

Only two of the universities – Nairobi and Mauritius – had units dedicated to coordinating the activities with external stakeholders (Box 6).

BOX 6

UNIVERSITY CONNECTEDNESS TO EXTERNAL GROUPINGS

External stakeholders involved in curriculum design

At the University of Mauritius, faculties and departments are required to engage advisory committees, which include external stakeholders from the public and private sectors and NGOs, around the development of new academic programmes and revisions to curricula. At the University of Botswana, every department has an advisory board which informs curriculum development. These boards comprise members of the department as well as key stakeholders from outside of the university (e.g. government, the private sector and NGOs).

Coordination of consultancy and other engagement activities

The University of Nairobi Enterprises and Services (UNES) Ltd was established in 1996 with the aim of promoting and coordinating the various income-generating activities of the university, including teaching, research and consultancy activities. UNES is registered as a private company, limited by shares, and operates as a separate legal entity, independent of the university. Amongst other things, UNES is responsible for promoting, coordinating and providing managerial services for income-generating activities within the university.

The key unit in the University of Mauritius for coordinating linkages and activities with government and industry is the Centre for Consultancy and Contract Research. The centre aims to encourage and facilitate consultancy activities amongst staff as a way of contributing to the socio-economic development of the country. It coordinates all consultancy and contract research, and manages intellectual property generated by university research, licensing and technology transfers. The centre's Consultancy Watch Unit was established in 2006 to assist staff to identify and develop consultancy opportunities.

FINDINGS

- While there is evidence of connectedness between the university and industry or the private sector in all eight universities, this is generally confined to the level of units or centres rather than institutional-level partnerships.
- Except for ad hoc consultancies at NMMU and Mauritius, there is virtually no evidence of university engagement in R&D with, or for, industry.

4.2.2   Foreign donors

Development aid contributed to the development of post-independence universities in Africa. However, as was discussed in the introduction (section 1.1), aid diminished dramatically during the 1980s and 1990s following the World Bank policy shift to primary education, and as relations between governments and universities deteriorated.

Development aid to higher education in Africa picked up again significantly in the post-2000 period. The CHET development aid study (Maassen *et al.* 2007) estimated that about USD 1 billion was donated to higher education in Africa during the 2000–2005 period. This new interest was considerably strengthened at the G8 Gleneagles summit (July 2005) where Africa and the Millennium Development Goals were the major focus. Following the summit, the office of the British prime minister issued a communiqué proclaiming an 'historic opportunity' and 'a renewed commitment': 'This is a moment of opportunity for Africa. Its leaders have embraced a new vision for the continent's future which recognises their leading role in addressing the continent's challenges and realising its opportunities' (G8 Gleneagles 2005: 11). The prime minister urged a focus on Africa because it 'is the only continent not on track to meet any of the goals of the Millennium Declaration by 2015' (ibid.).

The summit made a pledge to increase annual Official Development Assistance to Africa by USD 22.6 billion by 2010. As the G8 accounts for 70% of all Official Development Assistance spending, this increase would more than double G8 aid to Africa. Specific goals included massive investments in education, and HIV and poverty reduction, which could have constituted a major push towards achieving the Millennium Development Goals.

According to an independent assessment of the G8 'promises to Africa' (Gastfriend & Morton 2010), 'the G8 is on track to deliver 61% of the Gleneagles commitments by 2010, an increase of approximately USD 13.7 billion per year [of the 22.6 billion promised]. The bulk of the shortfall falls on three countries: France, Germany and Italy', while 'by the end of 2010 Japan, the US and Canada will have exceeded their commitments' and the UK is expected to almost fulfil its promises. So, while not living up to the ambitious pledge of 2005, substantial amounts of funds are going into development aid, and there is a renewed interest in higher education.

A reading of the main international declarations and agreements on development aid in Africa shows widely divergent approaches, with no generally accepted 'development model' or approach that links a set of key drivers for development. This is probably owing to the particularity of the national interests of the participating countries. But, in Africa, there is also no agreement on the role of higher education in development aid. For example, the Economic Commission for Africa (ECA) produced a weighty tome in 2004 entitled *Economic Report on Africa – Unlocking Africa's trade potential*. There is no reference in this highly publicised document regarding the role of higher education and its importance for knowledge creation, skills development and development in general (Maassen *et al.* 2007). A similar lack of focus on higher education characterises the official documents of the New Partnership for Africa's Development (NEPAD) and the Southern African Development Community (SADC).

Even if the G8 has only managed to meet 61% of its target, it still amounts to a substantial increase in development aid to Africa in general, and to higher education in particular, and to significant amounts of funds. The issue is thus not only about more aid, but importantly how to spend the aid more effectively. In the context of this study, our interest in the relationship between foreign aid and higher education in Africa has three dimensions. These include agenda-setting, the coordination of aid projects, and the possible effects of development aid on the academic cores of African universities.

According to institutional leaders at the University of Dar es Salaam, not all donor agencies take the government's priorities into account, while others do. The Swedish agency Sida was mentioned as a particular example of a big donor that responds to proposals from local demand. Some interviewees suggested that donors are more likely to push their own agendas with individual academics. For example, one respondent said that 'there are those donors who have special agendas and they will always go to a particular member of staff or a particular head of department'.

At the University of Ghana, a number of respondents spoke about the tensions between responding to the agendas of foreign donors in order to secure research or project funding, on the one hand, and addressing local needs, on the other. For example, one project leader talked about the difficulties of raising funds for new health problems such as chronic high blood pressure, heart disease and diabetes when donors only want to fund research into tropical (malaria) and infectious (HIV/Aids) diseases. Another highlighted the tension between donor and country priorities, as well as traditional forms of academic assessment.

Some senior academics also commented on the changing of, and increasing lack of clarity about, what donors want to fund, particularly in the social sciences. In the words of a senior academic at the University of Nairobi: 'I'm not sure I know what the donors are interested in. I don't mind ideology, even if I don't agree with it, at least I know where I stand, but with many of the major donors I don't know anymore where I stand – for the life of me I don't know who is funding the social sciences.'

Coordination of agendas and projects is a major problem, not to mention the considerable administrative effort required for accounting to multiple donors. At some institutions the data collected and formatted for donor reports were much more systematic and organised than the data for government or institutional management.

Two universities where considerable effort and resources have been put into donor coordination are Dar es Salaam and Eduardo Mondlane (Box 7). According to the Director of Planning and Finance at Dar es Salaam, they are trying to move towards institutionalising the strategic plan in terms of foreign donor funding that comes into the university. This is only beginning to be possible now since, in the past, the institution's needs were so many that they would accept any money that was offered:

> *You know, when you have so many needs – we have deteriorating students' hostels, we don't have enough teaching facilities, the laboratories are dead, the workshops are dead. You see, wherever you get funds you tend to say: yes, please give me because I'm in need of this. But I think now given what we have received in terms of a loan from the World Bank support, we can now say: [ ] these are the areas that we now need support, in the next five years.*

The director also reported that while there is some coordination between donor agencies at a national level (e.g. where donors are aware of what other donors are funding at the government level), there is no coordination in terms of what is being funded in the university (as the money is channelled via the national treasury):

> *It was very interesting to see, with just two more partners we could see already there was no coordination. They didn't know each other and they were overlapping some activities. So it made us realise that it's very urgent and important to have this horizontal dialogue, not just vertical dialogue. I mean, the donors communicate with us but they don't communicate with each other.*

At Eduardo Mondlane, the newly established Donor Coordination Unit, which reports directly to the vice-chancellor, is responsible for coordinating institutional and foreign donor interests and agendas. This unit emerged out of the long-standing unit responsible for coordination of the Sida/SAREC[12] cooperation. The unit at Eduardo Mondlane will also be responsible for bringing together major donors to meet and discuss their activities in order to coordinate funding areas and reporting mechanisms, and to avoid duplication or overlap where possible. However, the unit's coordinator reported that at a recent meeting of large donors, it was evident that there was little coordination between them in terms of funding areas and activities and it is virtually impossible to ensure coordination with the smaller donor-funded projects since these are usually negotiated with individual researchers.

---

12   SAREC is the Department for Research Cooperation of Sida, the Swedish International Development Cooperation Agency.

Eduardo Mondlane University, which has probably received the largest proportion of donor aid amongst the universities in our sample, has had a more than 30-year relationship with Sida/SAREC in addition to large development grants from the World Bank via the government. Over this period, Sida/SAREC has funded individual projects, capacity development (including masters and PhD degrees), bigger research programmes and a facilities fund which covers expensive equipment and the maintenance of laboratories and so on. Over the past few years, it has been mandatory to include masters and PhD training in the larger research programmes funded by Sida.

However, although there has been an increase in enrolments in masters programmes at Eduardo, their doctoral enrolments are the weakest in the sample of eight countries (Table 3). This is partially due to the fact that many doctoral candidates still enrol at overseas universities, particularly in the donor countries, but more importantly because there is no coordinated triangle of government, university and donor support. Government has abdicated the contribution to research and doctoral training to donors. But donors cannot be a 'surrogate state': training at the highest level and knowledge production at a globally competitive level requires concentrated effort from the government, donors and the university.

BOX 7

CONNECTING INTERNAL UNIVERSITY AND EXTERNAL DONOR INTERESTS

At Eduardo Mondlane University, the newly established Donor Coordination Unit, which reports directly to the vice-chancellor, is responsible for coordinating institutional and foreign donor interests and agendas. This includes negotiating with the larger donors that the programmes funded are aligned with both institutional and national priorities. The unit will also be responsible for bringing major donors together to discuss their activities with a view to coordinating funding areas and reporting mechanisms.

The key coordinating body at the University of Dar es Salaam is the Department of Planning and Finance. The department coordinates planning and implementation of the strategic plan in various units, raises funds from different sources, and oversees the income and expenditure on these funds. Of particular interest to this study is the department's role in ensuring a degree of alignment between the institution's strategic objectives, academic activities and foreign donor interests.

FINDINGS

- The coordination of agendas and projects with donors is a major problem, not to mention the considerable administrative effort required for accounting to multiple donors. Only two institutions (Dar es Salaam and Eduardo Mondlane) had established strong coordination structures.
- Particularly amongst social scientists there is a perception of a decrease in donor interest, and an increasing lack of clarity about what donors want to fund.

4.3 The connectedness of development activities to the academic core

A key issue for the relationship between higher education and economic development is to establish a *productive* relationship between knowledge and connectedness. On the one hand, if there is an overemphasis on the basic knowledge activities of teaching and research – in other words, an excessive inward orientation towards strengthening the academic core – this results in the university becoming an 'ivory tower'. Or, if the academic core is weak, an overemphasis on knowledge results in the 'ancillary' role of the university (i.e. no direct role in development). On the other hand, an overemphasis in the university on connecting to development activities weakens the academic core and the university has little new or relevant knowledge to offer in the exchange relationship.

The challenge for universities, then, is to deal with this inherent tension between 'buffering' (protecting) the core technologies of the institution, and 'bridging' (linking) those with external actors (Scott 2001: 199–211). In reality, the boundaries between internal and external are not that clear cut. A number of higher education experts, such as Gibbons *et al.* (1994) and Scott (2001), have argued that with globalisation and its associated 'new' forms of knowledge production, the boundaries are becoming increasingly blurred and permeable.

The higher education studies literature describes this problem in terms of the conceptual notion of 'coupling' (Scott 2001; Weick 1976); that is, the extent to which the core and the external (or 'periphery') are linked with, or connected to, one another. In 'tight coupling', the boundary is weak and the university is in a direct, 'instrumental' relationship with external actors such as government or industry. In 'loose-coupling', the boundary is stronger, such as in the traditional notion of the university as a self-governing institution, which assumes an indirect contribution to development. The more complex relationship is with the 'engine of development' notion where there are multiple, simultaneous forms of knowledge production and exchange.

For the purposes of this study, we are using the term 'connectedness' to refer to the relationship (and tension) between the inward focus on strengthening and maintaining the academic core, and the outward focus on linking with external stakeholders and development. In this section, we present a methodology for investigating this tension and apply this methodology to a small selection of projects from the eight universities in the study.

We begin with a brief overview of the methodology employed in collecting and analysing the data in order to address these questions.

4.3.1 Methodology

In preparation for the research team's visit to each institution, institutional leaders were asked to identify five to ten development-related projects (i.e. with an economic development or poverty reduction focus) to include in the investigation. In the end, a wide range of information was gathered on 44 projects and centres across the eight universities. While these projects and centres might not necessarily constitute 'flagship' or 'exemplary' projects in every case, they are considered by university leadership to be strongly connected to development.

We operationalised 'connectedness' along two dimensions. The first dimension is 'articulation' which has a number of aspects. Firstly, it refers to the extent to which the aims and outcomes of development-related activities articulate with national development priorities and the university's strategic objectives. Secondly, it refers to the linkages the project has with two of the groups of stakeholders in the triangle – the government (usually through specific government departments or agencies) and external stakeholders (e.g. industry, small businesses, NGOs or community groups such as fishers or small-scale farmers). In particular, our focus is on the extent to which there are linkages with an 'implementation agency' (i.e. an external body which takes up the knowledge and/or its products generated or applied through research or training). Thirdly, articulation takes into account linkages generated through sources of funding in two respects: whether the project/centre obtains funding from one or more of the three stakeholder groups (government, an external funder or the university itself); and the extent to which the project/centre develops a relationship with its funders over time. This latter aspect is determined through the nature of the financial sustainability of the project.

The second dimension focuses on the extent to which development activities serve to 'strengthen the academic core' of the university. This was operationalised in terms of the extent to which the work undertaken in projects/centres feeds into teaching or curriculum development; is linked to the formal training of students; enables academics to publish in academic publications (journals, books etc); is linked to international academic networks; and generates new knowledge (versus applying existing knowledge).

These various aspects relating to 'articulation' and 'strengthening the academic core' were converted into indicators (Table 9) which could then be applied to an analysis of the development-related projects and centres included in the study. On the basis of the indicator ratings, the projects/centres were plotted on a graph depicting the intersection between 'articulation' and 'strengthening the academic core'. Detailed descriptions and analyses of the 44 projects/centres can be found in the eight case study reports which are available on the CHET website.

4.3.2 The project data and analysis

For the purposes of this synthesis report, one project or centre from each of the eight universities has been selected for analysis and discussion. Together, these projects/centres represent the spectrum of different types or categories, such as long-term research programmes or short-term consultancies, institutionalised training and small business support. Table 8 provides an overview of the eight projects/centres. Table 9 provides the summary 'articulation' and 'strengthening the academic core' ratings, respectively. The projects/centres are then plotted along the two axes in Figure 3.

TABLE 8 Overview of the development-related projects/centres

University	Project/centre	Classification	Timeframe	Funder(s)	Beneficiaries	Initiation/agenda-setting	Economic development focus
Botswana	UB Business Clinic (BC)	Practical training and support services	1995, ongoing	University, income generated through student businesses	Students and the public who want to start or grow their SMEs	Faculty staff	Support to establish new, or grow existing, SMEs
Dar es Salaam	SME Gatsby Clubs (SMEGC)	Small business support	2004, ongoing	Foreign donors, the university	SMEs in Tanzania	Staff in the university	Training, support and facilities to SMEs in target groups
Eduardo Mondlane	Energy, Environment and Climate Change (EECC)	Research programme	2006, ongoing	Foreign donors, government agency	Government, private sector, NGOs, students, people living in rural areas	Academic staff	Development of renewable energy solutions
Ghana	Noguchi Memorial Institute for Medical Research (NMIMR)	Research institute and postgraduate training programmes	1979, ongoing	Foreign donors, government	People of Ghana, government health agencies, local NGOs	Foreign donors, institute staff	Research, training and diagnostic services for the public health sector
Makerere	Community-Based Education and Service provision (COBES)	Community-based education and service provision	2003/2004, ongoing	Foreign donors, the university, some income generation	College of Health Sciences students, local communities	University staff	Healthcare provision to poor and rural communities
Mauritius	Review of Strategies for Poverty Alleviation (RPAS)	Externally-funded consultancy	February–October 2009	Independent consultative body to government	Government ministry	Consultative body	Inform policy-making and build capacity amongst stakeholders involved in poverty alleviation
Nairobi	African Collaborative Centre for Earth System Science (ACCESS)	Long-term research and capacity building programme	1989, ongoing	Government agency, the university, foreign donors	African science and policy communities, NGOs, local communities	University academic, international academic network	Research and capacity building around environmental issues that are linked to poverty
NMMU	Automotive Components Technology Station (ACTS)	Consultancy projects and training	2002, ongoing	Government agency, income generation	SMEs in the automotive components industry	Academics with industry experience, donor	Consultancy projects and training for industry (especially SMEs)

TABLE 9 Development projects/centres: 'Articulation' and 'strengthening the academic core' ratings

Projects/centres	UB Business Clinic	SME Gatsby Clubs	Energy, Environment and Climate Change	Noguchi Memorial Institute for Medical Research	Community-Based Education and Service	Review of Strategies for Poverty Alleviation	African Collaborative Centre for Earth System Science	Automotive Components Technology Station
ARTICULATION RATING (maximum score = 13)								
Institutional objectives	2	2	0	0	0	0	0	2
National priorities	1	2	2	2	1	2	1	2
Number of funding source(s)	2	2	2	2	3	1	3	2
Funding sustainability	3	2	2	3	2	1	3	3
Implementation agency	0	2	1	2	0	1	1	2
Total articulation rating	**8**	**10**	**7**	**9**	**6**	**5**	**8**	**11**
STRENGTHENING ACADEMIC CORE RATING (maximum score = 5)								
Teaching/curriculum development	0	0	1	1	1	1	1	1
Formal training of students	0	1	1	1	1	0	1	1
Generate new knowledge	0	0	1	1	0	1	1	1
Academic publications	0	0	1	1	1	0	1	1
Link to international academic networks	0	0	1	1	0	0	1	1
Total academic core rating	**0**	**1**	**5**	**5**	**3**	**2**	**5**	**5**

'Articulation' key:
- Institutional objectives/National priorities:
  2 = Direct (link to specific strategic objective or national priority)
  1 = Indirect (broad/general reference)
  0 = None (no reported link)
- Number of funding sources:
  1 for each of the following: University; Government; Foreign donor; Income generation
- Funding sustainability:
  1 = Once-off, short-term (a project that is one year or less in duration and which receives only one round of funding)
  2 = Long-term but capped (a project that is more than one year in duration and which receives one or more rounds of funding, but the funding is capped)
  3 = Ongoing (a project which receives ongoing funding, e.g. from the university or from income generation)
- Link to implementation agency:
  2 = Direct
  1 = Indirect
  0 = None

'Strengthening the academic core' key: 1 = Yes   0 = No

FIGURE 3 Plotting the development activities

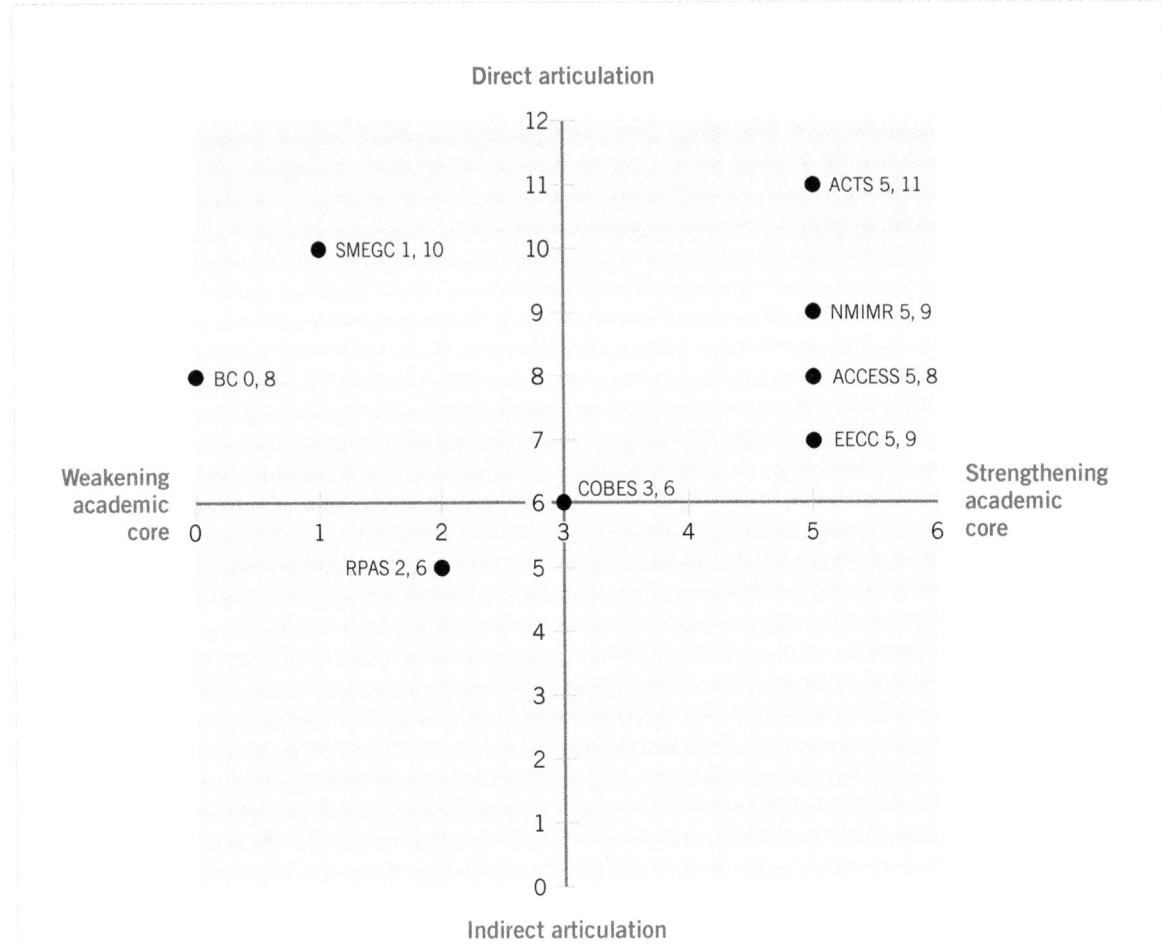

Key:

Abbreviation	Project/centre	University
BC	UB Business Clinic	Botswana
SMEGC	SME Gatsby Clubs	Dar es Salaam
EECC	Energy, Environment and Climate Change Research Programme	Eduardo Mondlane
NMIMR	Noguchi Memorial Institute for Medical Research	Ghana
RPAS	Review of Poverty Alleviation Strategies	Mauritius
ACCESS	African Collaborative Centre for Earth System Science	Nairobi
ACTS	Automotive Components Technology Station	Nelson Mandela Metropolitan
COBES	Community-Based Education and Service	Makerere

4.3.3 Discussion

In terms of our analysis, which focuses on the interaction between the articulation of these projects with external stakeholders and strengthening the academic core of the institution, the projects/centres fall into three groups.

The first group are those which fall within the top right-hand quadrant of the graph, which indicates that they score strongly on both the articulation and academic core axes. There were examples of such projects/centres in all eight universities in the study. In practice, this means that these projects/centres have found a way of balancing the potential tensions between the two objectives of articulating to external stakeholders whilst also strengthening the core knowledge activities of the institution. On the one hand, projects/centres such as the Automotive Components Technology Station, the Noguchi Memorial Institute for Medical Research (NMIMR), the African Collaborative Centre for Earth System Science (ACCESS) and the Energy, Environment and Climate Change Research Programme reflect specific national development priorities in their aims and objectives; have more than one funding source and plans for financial sustainability; and have links to one or more implementation agencies. On the other hand, the work of these projects/centres provides opportunities for the formal training of students, feeds into teaching and curriculum development, generates new knowledge and academic publications, and has linkages to international academic networks.

A second group of projects/centres are those which fall somewhere within the middle of the graph, indicating that while they are connected to external stakeholders in some respects, and go some way towards strengthening the academic core, they are not strong on either. The example in the selected projects above is the Community-Based Education and Service.

The third group, which contains the smallest number of projects/centres, mostly falls within the top-left quadrant of the graph. These projects/centres are often well-connected to external stakeholders via funding or implementation agencies, but they score poorly on the academic core axis, meaning that although they are making a contribution to development, they are not strengthening the core knowledge activities of the university. Amongst the selected projects highlighted above, the three examples of this include UB Business Clinic, the SME Gatsby Clubs and the short-term consultancy project on Reviewing Poverty Alleviation Strategies – all of which are disconnected from the academic core.

The first observation is that these projects/centres were chosen by the institutional leadership as cases of their university's contribution to development. What we could not ascertain, owing to a lack of information, is how many short-term consultancy projects there are and how connected/disconnected these are to development goals and the strengthening of the academic core. Doing an indepth case study of a sample of institutions would be very illuminating in this regard.

The second observation is that the development activities which scored high on articulation and strengthening the academic core are world-class. To mention two: ACCESS at the University of Nairobi is a multi-funded centre of excellence that plays a significant role in the United Nations Framework Convention on Climate Change, while having postgraduate students and fellows from all over the world. The NMIMR in Ghana, co-funded by the Japanese government for 30 years, is a leading biomedical research and training centre in communicable diseases that also performs national health laboratory services. In terms of sustainability, the only difference between the two centres is that the NMIMR is very institutionalised, with successive directors coming from the faculty, while ACCESS seems much more dependent on one exceptional individual. The problem in our sample is that there are simply not enough of these activities that are connected to both development goals and the academic core.

FINDINGS

- Projects/centres that are considered by university leadership to be strongly connected to development tend to score well on the articulation indicators – in other words, they reflect national priorities (and to a lesser extent institutional objectives), have more than one funding source and, in some cases, plans for financial sustainability, and may have a connection to an implementation agency.
- A number of these projects/centres also manage to keep a strong connection to the academic core of the university, whilst others are virtually disconnected from these core knowledge activities.
- At each of the universities there are 'exemplary' development projects/centres. The problem is scale: there are simply not enough, and some seem overly-dependent on exceptional individuals.

Chapter 5

Conclusions and some implications

Three years of HERANA research into the role of universities in economic development in Africa, including surveys of three successful innovation-driven OECD countries and eight African nations and universities, produced an analytical framework to explore the role of universities in (economic) development and how this role might be operationalised. It also produced the most comprehensive, systematic and comparative data on a group of sub-Saharan African universities ever compiled.

The research led to key findings in three broad areas, the needs: for a 'pact' that sees governments, universities, funders and other stakeholders agree on a central role for higher education in economic development and the knowledge economy; for strengthening the 'academic core' of universities that is essential to producing knowledge, reproducing the academy and providing the high-level skills that drive development; and for improving policy (and implementation) coordination at national and institutional levels in ways that help to connect universities more effectively to development.

KEY FINDINGS

- There is a lack of clarity and agreement (pact) about a development model and the role of higher education in development, at both national and institutional levels. There is, however, an increasing awareness, particularly at government level, of the importance of universities in the global context of the knowledge economy.
- Research production at the eight African universities is not strong enough to enable them to build on their traditional undergraduate teaching roles and make a sustainable, comprehensive contribution to development via new knowledge production. A number of universities have manageable student–staff ratios and adequately qualified staff, but inadequate funds for staff to engage in research. In addition, the incentive regimes do not support knowledge production.
- In none of the countries in the sample is there a coordinated effort between government, external stakeholders and the university to systematically strengthen the contribution that the university can make to development. While at each of the universities there are exemplary development projects that connect strongly to external stakeholders and strengthen the academic core, the challenge is how to increase the number of these projects.

5.1   Pact needed on 'engine for development' role for universities

The development model of the three OECD systems studied in this project represents what the WEF competitiveness report classifies as 'innovation-driven' – in other words, these countries have agreed that knowledge and education are key productive factors in development. From the sample of eight African countries, three (Mauritius, South Africa and Botswana) are in the 'efficiency' phase, meaning that improved efficiency and higher education and training are increasingly playing an important role in economic development. The other countries are in the process of moving from 'factor' (natural resources and low skills base) towards efficiency and, by implication, an increasing importance for education and training.

This study revealed that the three efficiency-driven systems already have substantially higher participation rates in higher education but that, with the exception of Mauritius, none of the countries has a consistent development model, nor is there agreement that knowledge is a key productive factor. In the rest of the sample there are emerging knowledge policies, but they are located mainly in one government department, with weak coordination and implementation.

In most of the countries in the sample, as a kind of compensation for the absence of a development model, grand, national visions are constructed. These visions, some looking forward as far as 2030, have no implementation plans or systematic monitoring mechanisms. To some extent they could be seen as attempts at constructing a common vision – and by implication confirming that there is no pact.

Mauritius is the only country where, at both the national and institutional levels, there is a belief that knowledge is a key driver of development, and where the government and the institution have similar notions about the role of the university. However, in terms of the academic core, coordination and implementation it does not seem as if the pact has been properly operationalised as yet.

The lack of the pact in our sample countries is also evidenced by the lack of consensus between national and university stakeholders around the role of higher education and universities. Amongst national stakeholders, the dominant expectation is that universities make a direct contribution to development. This instrumental notion emphasises contribution in the form of expertise exchange and capacity building, rather than the production of new scientific knowledge. It is a constant refrain from government stakeholders that universities are not contributing enough to development; however, this is usually in reference to addressing broad social problems rather than to economic development in particular.

On the whole, national stakeholders and some government policies and plans reflect the language of the knowledge economy and the role of the university as the 'engine of development' – more so than university stakeholders and plans do. However, it is likely that this is still a more instrumental notion of knowledge since it is used in the sense of direct application to development issues rather than the more indirect role of knowledge and universities in R&D and innovation.

It is surprising that amongst university leadership, support for the role of the university in the knowledge economy is rather weak. Instead, the two dominant notions reflect the traditional tension between the university as a self-governing institution that indirectly contributes to development, versus a more direct instrumental role. There is an emerging awareness of the importance of an 'engine of development' approach in the sample but, with the exception of Mauritius, it is far from being the dominant view.

In the period following independence in many African countries, a clear pact developed between government and universities that universities would provide the human capital (civil service and professions) for the new states. That pact is long gone. Instead, there are a range of policy visions and notions, often contradictory, within government and within universities about how to respond to changing development demands that are increasingly driven by knowledge. What has not changed is that there is, with the exception of Mauritius, not a generally agreed upon development model, with the result that neither the government nor institutions agree on the role of higher education in development.

It could thus be argued that there needs to be considerably more emphasis on 'forging' agreement between governments, funders and university leaders that knowledge and higher education are key productive forces. So while capacity-building is important, consensus-building is equally important – capacity-building without agreement on 'capacity for what' may be part of the 'bottomless pit' syndrome in Africa.

A potentially positive development in terms of forging greater agreement across different constituencies is that in all the countries, tertiary or higher education councils have been established, partially to compensate for weak ministries but also to do 'independent' certification and quality assessments. Currently they are partially 'symptoms' of problems in the system, but all are undergoing 'role re-definitions' and could become key players in promoting discussions about the role of higher education in development and in monitoring progress.

5.2 Strengthening the academic core – incentives are key

The university is a specialised institution whose core business is knowledge – its production, reproduction and dissemination. In addition, the university can only participate in the global knowledge economy and make a sustainable contribution to development if its 'academic core' is strong. The core knowledge production output variables of the sample African universities are not strong enough for them to make a sustainable contribution to development, and the academic core indicators do not show significant signs of strengthening knowledge production outputs (doctorates and publications).

As was the case with the European university tradition before the second world war, and until fairly recently the Latin American model (Swartzman 2010), the universities in our sample are still predominantly organised as undergraduate teaching institutions, despite some rather grandiose mission statements and claims to be knowledge producers. But just as was the case in Europe, Latin America and Asia, the challenges facing African universities are to expand their role beyond teaching to research and to become significant contributors to what Douglass *et al.* (2009: 1) call 'globalisation's muse': 'Universities and higher education systems, for both real and romanticised reasons have become globalisation's muse: in essence a widely recognised route to full participation in the knowledge society.'

The convergence in weakness of research output is in contrast to much greater variance in input strengths. The strongest input indicators are in manageable student-staff ratios and the relatively high level of staff with PhDs, which could partially account for solid undergraduate success rates. However, these success rates have to be seen within the context of the combination of a flagship university in a national system of low participation rates, meaning a very elite group of students.

The two areas of greatest concern on the input side are the low levels of postgraduate students, particularly at the doctorate level, and the lack of research funds. A striking feature of postgraduate enrolment is the dramatic increase in masters enrolments and graduations. There are two sides to this. On the one hand, course work masters degrees certainly contribute to increasing the pool of highly-skilled workers beyond the bachelor degree, which is a feature of many knowledge economies. On the other hand, these mainly course work masters programmes do not seem to prepare students for doctoral studies, particularly the research and dissertation components. Very poor throughput rates – in some cases, more than 50 masters students for every PhD enrolment – attest to this. But there could also be other contributing factors, such as the fact that there are many more scholarships for masters programmes, particularly from foreign donors, while scholarships for doctoral studies are much scarcer.

Not enrolling and graduating PhDs has a number of serious consequences. Firstly, the flagship university has to reproduce its own academic staff, as well as academics for other higher education institutions in the system. It also has to respond to the increasing demand in the knowledge economy for people with doctorates in institutions other than the university, such as research institutes, and for high-level person power in top positions in a range of industrial and financial institutions.

New knowledge production and connecting university research to application and innovation is most frequently led by academic staff with doctorates and research programmes. The vast majority of the development activities identified by university leadership for the study were led by academics with PhDs. Growing the cadre of doctorates is an essential task for a flagship university – not only to reproduce itself, but also to produce knowledge that can connect the institution to both the global knowledge economy and the local community.

'ISI-referenced publications' represents a narrow notion of research which does not reflect research that feeds into application or consultancy, and could thus be seen as only the tip of the 'research iceberg'. However, this is the tip that makes a flagship university part of the global knowledge community, and publishing part of an international disciplinary or inter-disciplinary community. Three crucial components of what might be called an output-oriented research culture that produces the 'tip' are: staff with appropriate research training (having a PhD is an essential but not sufficient requirement), research funding, and a conducive incentive environment.

The first problem with the incentive structure at the university level starts with the problem of very little earmarked research funding coming from government, which puts pressure on universities to find incentive money from their already-stretched budgets. While almost every university has a research fund, the funds have to be shared with related activities such as conference attendance, equipment and information resources. In addition, it seems that most of these internal 'open competitive' funding sources are mainly incentives for young academics and doctoral students, with many senior academics saying that the amounts available are not worth applying for. A related problem, in some cases, is that while some money is available for equipment, it is nearly impossible to get equipment maintenance funds.

The second problem with the incentives structure is that it seems a major distraction from PhD supervision and academic research for some staff is multiple private teaching opportunities, both within public institutions with 'private' students and in private higher education institutions located in close proximity to the flagship institution. So while the teaching load, according to student-staff ratios, might not be excessive, this 'triple teaching' as a form of income supplementation is another contributor to weakening the academic core.

A third potential problem is related to consultancies for government, foreign donors and industry. While most academics interviewed mentioned consultancies, it is very difficult to get anything near an accurate picture of consultancy activity. (In one of the Dar es Salaam annual reports a figure of about 800 consultancies was mentioned.) Nevertheless, what emerged from these discussions is that consultancies have major advantages over research grants. Firstly, it is a personal relationship with a donor that often also has other benefits such as travelling to the donor country and being invited to networks of other recipients. Secondly, consultancies provide both direct supplementation of income and have much greater flexibility about how the funds are spent (whereas research grants often have numerous stipulations about travel, hiring of researchers, buying of equipment, etc).

It is clear from this investigation that in order to 'refocus' universities, attention will have to be paid to incentive structures that promote knowledge production. Low knowledge production cannot be blamed solely on low capacity and resources. What needs to be incentivised is PhD supervision and research programmes that strengthen the academic core, make these flagship universities part of the global academic community, and connect them to local and regional development.

Part of developing the academic core will be to improve and strengthen the definition of key performance indicators, as well as the systematic, institution-wide capturing and processing (institutionalisation) of key performance indicator data. Such indicators will be key for national and institutional decision-makers to design evidence-based policies and incentives, rather than the current over-reliance on aspirational mission statements.

5.3 Coordination and connectedness to development

The university cannot unilaterally strengthen the academic core and connect it to development-related activities. It requires the coordination of government policies and other external stakeholders. At the national level, there were considerable coordination activities in most countries, ranging from forums and clusters to the reorganisation of national ministries. However, this seemed to be mostly weak or 'symbolic' coordination.

Evidence of this was not only in the lack of supporting policies across relevant departments, but also in the focus of such policies often being contingent on the interests of different and changing government ministers. This was reflected, amongst others ways, in the fact that policies to support research were often in departments of science and technology, but not in education. Another indicator was the reconfiguration of ministries of education, either separating higher education from basic education, linking and delinking higher education from science and technology, or even linking higher education to training.

In the absence of a pact, and with competing notions and a lack of consensus between universities, national authorities and external actors about the university's identity and its role in development, coordination becomes virtually impossible. A consequence is that the energy and actions of university leaders and academics have to be invested in continuous, unpredictable negotiations, particularly about funding from government – instead of in strengthening the core academic activities of the institution. The result of this is often fragmented and inefficient organisations characterised by intra-organisational struggles for power, autonomy and funding.

The above can be illustrated by looking at research funding. In all eight countries there are national policies that promote research and innovation, but these are mostly located within science and technology departments, not in education (with the exception of Botswana and Mauritius). Funding from government through education departments is mainly for teaching and infrastructure, with between 1–3% available for research at most institutions. Academics often described their government's contribution to research funds as 'negligible'.[13]

In all the countries studied dissatisfaction was expressed with the national research councils: not only are the amounts of money limited, but funds are cumbersome to access through complicated application procedures, and grants are often for short periods, meaning repeated reapplication.

In the absence of a coordinated funding and incentive strategy from government, reliance on external funding increases which, in turn, can contribute to more fragmentation and 'projectisation'. This weakens the academic core of universities because knowledge is not accumulated and fed into teaching and publishing, and the entire system is more vulnerable to donor agendas, interventions and political interference.

---

13   According to Oyewole (2010), on average, sub-Saharan African countries spend less than 0.3% of their GDP on research – the lowest in the world. Furthermore, Africa has lost 11% of its share of global science since its peak in 1987, while sub-Saharan science has lost almost a third (31%).

Although donor aid in Africa has not reached the ambitious targets set at the 2005 G8 summit, reaching about 60% of the targets still amounts to a significant increase in development aid to Africa in general, and to higher education in particular. The issue is not only about more aid but, equally importantly, how to spend the aid more effectively.

This study shows that the coordination of agendas and projects with donors is a major problem, not to mention the considerable administrative effort required for accounting to multiple donors. Only two institutions (Dar es Salaam and Eduardo Mondlane) had established strong donor coordination structures. But, as was indicated in the case of Eduardo Mondlane, to strengthen the academic core requires coordination and a joint effort by donors and government; research and doctoral training cannot be 'outsourced' to donors while government funds undergraduate teaching.

One way to start addressing the serious shortage and lack of coordination of national and continental research funds, is to consider an African version of the recently established European Research Council, a body that concentrates large amounts of funds to promote frontier research excellence.

Strengthening the academic core not only requires more research funds but also mechanisms that connect the university to development activities in ways that strengthen rather than weaken the academic core. Starting with industry linkages, while there was evidence of connecting to industry or the private sector in all eight universities, this was generally confined to the level of units or centres rather than institutional-level partnerships. Except for ad hoc consultancies at some universities, there was virtually no evidence of university engagement in R&D with, or for, industry.

To a large extent this is because the industrial sector in most of the African countries studied is largely under-developed, and because there is very limited private sector R&D – where global companies do have operations in the African countries, their R&D is usually undertaken elsewhere. This is a problem in most developing countries but it is particularly acute in Africa. However, some of the universities are beginning to address the lack of interaction between their institutions and industry or the private sector through the establishment of university-industry liaison structures.

Interaction with the private sector took mainly two forms. The first is in the area of education and training. Examples include the use of people from the private sector on advisory committees responsible for curricula design and revision, for work placements, and for specific, customised training programmes. The second form of interaction, at almost all the universities, is business development and support for SMEs. A challenge will be to increase the scale of these initiatives while still connecting them to research and postgraduate training, because these types of projects lend themselves to individual consultancies.

The survey of 44 projects/centres identified by university leaders as being strongly connected to development, ranged from long-term research programmes to postgraduate training and short-term support services to external groupings. At each of the universities there are 'exemplary' development projects/centres that are strongly connected to national/ local priorities, have more than one funding source and, in some cases, have a connection to an implementation agency. At the same time, they are strengthening the academic core through training postgraduate students, are part of international academic networks, and have published in peer-reviewed journals and books. A few projects are world class in terms of international recognition and cutting-edge research (particularly in the areas of the environment and health). The challenge is to vastly increase the number and the scale of these types of projects.

Finally, our approach to higher education and development can be illustrated by a version of the Burton Clark 'coordination triangle'. Clark's seminal book *The Higher Education System* (1983) addressed the issue of the organisation of higher education systems and argued that factors that integrate higher education systems (i.e. that keep them from falling apart) are the three forces of coordination: the state, the market and the academic oligarchy. These form the three nodes in his triangle.

In the context of this study, we have adapted Clark's triangle (Figure 4) to depict the three main nodes as government, universities and external groupings. These in turn reflect the dynamics of our analytical framework which can be articulated as follows: in order for universities to make a sustainable contribution to development, there needs to be agreement amongst the major actors (a pact) about the role of development; there needs to be capacity in the academic core of universities; and there needs to be coordination and connectedness of the policies and activities of government, universities and external groupings.

These three aspects are interrelated. Without a pact, coordination becomes virtually impossible. Without national policies and implementation of these policies, it is very difficult for the university to develop a strong academic core (particularly in developing countries where the market is weak). But, strong academic capacity without being connected to development activities results in the insulation of the university (the 'ivory tower'). Strong connectedness of universities to development, but with weak academic capacity, diminishes the contribution the university can make to development.

The above does not mean that there is one best practice model to achieve this. Our study of the three systems that have been successful in different ways in connecting higher education to development (Finland, South Korea and North Carolina) showed this.

For African countries to move from being providers of raw materials and receivers of foreign aid to the next stages of development that will make them part of the global knowledge economy, implies at least the following. Firstly, agreement (a pact) about the importance of knowledge in development and the special role of the university. Secondly, strengthening the academic core, particularly in terms of knowledge production. Thirdly, greater coordination amongst an increasing number of actors and agencies (multiple government departments, business and foreign donors) involved in higher education. And finally, ensuring that development activities strengthen rather than weaken academic capacity, particularly for flagship universities.

FIGURE 4 **The dynamics of the relationship between the pact, academic core and coordination**

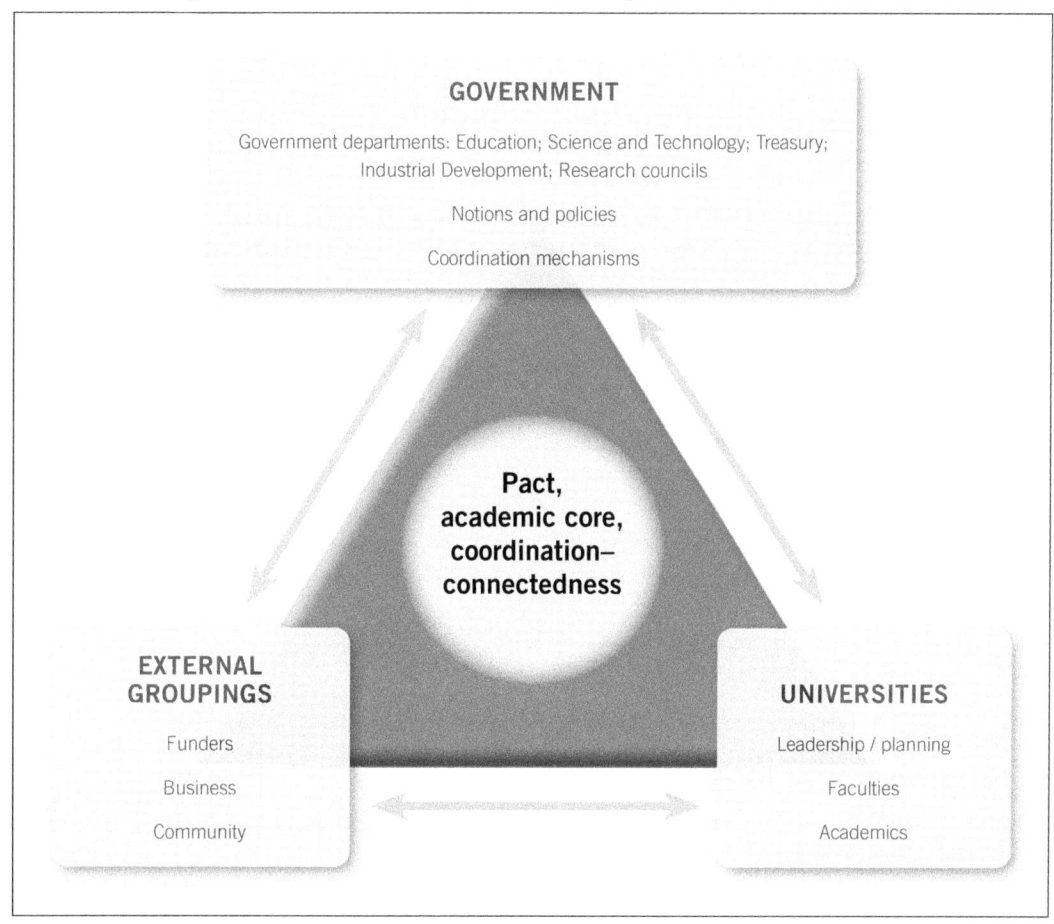

List of sources

Altbach PG and Balán J (eds) (2007) *World Class Worldwide: Transforming research universities in Asia and Latin America.* Baltimore: The Johns Hopkins University Press

Bloom D, Canning D and Chan K (2006) *Higher Education and Economic Development in Africa.* Washington DC: The World Bank

Braun D (2008) Organising the political coordination of knowledge and innovation policies. *Science and Public Policy,* 35(4): 227–239

Brock-Utne B (2002) Formulating higher education policies in Africa: The pressure from external forces and the neo-liberal agenda. *Journal of Higher Education in Africa,* (1)1: 24–56

Carnoy M, Castells M, Cohen SS and Cardoso FH (1993) *The New Global Economy in the Information Age: Reflections on our changing world.* University Park: Pennsylvania State University Press

Castells M (1991) *The University System: Engine of development in the new world economy.* Washington DC: The World Bank

Castells M (2002) Universities as dynamic systems of contradictory functions. In: Muller J, Cloete N and Badat S (eds) *Challenges of Globalisation: South African debates with Manuel Castells.* Cape Town: Maskew Miller Longman

Castells M (2009) Transcript of a lecture on higher education delivered at the University of the Western Cape, 7 August 2009. http://www.chet.org.za/seminars/

CHET (2010) *Cross-national higher education performance indicators.* Draft report. Cape Town: Centre for Higher Education Transformation

Clark B (1983) *The Higher Education System: Academic organization in cross-national perspective.* Berkeley: University of California Press

Clark B (1998) *Creating Entrepreneurial Universities: Organisational pathways of transformation.* Oxford: Pergamon-IAU Press

Coleman J and Court D (1993) *University Development in the Third World: The Rockefeller experience.* New York: Pergamon

Douglass JA, King CJ and Feller I (2009) *Globalization's Muse: Universities and higher education systems in a changing world.* Berkeley: Public Policy Press, Center for Studies in Higher Education, Institute of Governmental Studies

Economic Report on Africa (2004) *Unlocking Africa's Trade Potential in the Global Economy Overview.* Twenty-third meeting of the Committee of Experts of the Conference of African Ministers of Finance, Planning and Economic Development, Kampala, Uganda. http://www.uneca.org/cfm/2004/overview.htm

French Academy of Sciences (2006) *Science and Developing Countries: Sub-Saharan Africa.* Paris.

G8 Gleneagles (2005) *The Gleneagles Communiqué.* http://www.chet.org.za/files/reports/Gleneagles_Communique_Africa.pdf

Gastfriend D and Morton R (2010) Promises and plans: An analysis of G8 aid to Africa. *International Institute for Justice and Development (IIJD) Newsletter,* July 2010. http://www.iijd.org/

Gibbons M, Limoges C, Nowotny H, Schwartsman S, Scott P and Trow M (1994) *The New Production of Knowledge: The dynamics of science and research in contemporary societies*. California: Sage Publications

Gornitzka Å, Maassen P, Olsen JP and Stensaker B (2007) 'Europe of knowledge': Search for a new pact. In: P Maassen and JP Olsen (eds), *University Dynamics and European Integration*. Dordrecht: Springer

Hölttä S and Malkki P (2000) *Response of Finnish higher education institutions to the national information society programme*. Helsinki University of Technology

Juma C and Yee-Cheong L (2005) *Innovation: Applying knowledge in development*. London: Earthscan

Kamara A and Nyende L (2007) Growing a Knowledge-Based Economy: Public expenditure on education in Africa. *Economic Research Working Paper,* No. 88. Tunisia: African Development Bank

Langa PV (2010) Disciplines and engagement in African universities: A study of scientific capital and academic networking in the social sciences. Unpublished PhD Dissertation, University of Cape Town

Maassen P and Cloete N (2006) Global reform trends in higher education. In: N Cloete, R Fehnel, P Maassen, T Moja, H Perold and T Gibbon (eds), *Transformation in Higher Education: Global pressures and local realities*. Second edition. Dordrecht: Springer

Maassen P, Pinheiro R and Cloete N (2007) *Bilateral country investments and foundations partnership projects to support higher education across Africa*. Report commissioned by the US Partnership for Higher Education in Africa. Cape Town: Centre for Higher Education Transformation

Maassen P and Olsen J (2007) University dynamics and European integration. *Higher Education Dynamics*, 19

MacGregor K (2009a) 'Conference calls for higher education action.' *University World News,* 22 July 2009
http://www.universityworldnews.com/article.php?story=20090709193555377

MacGregor K (2009b) 'Africa: Call for higher education support fund.' *University World News,* 22 July 2009
http://www.universityworldnews.com/article.php?story=20090322082237425

MacGregor K (2010) 'Higher education a driver of the MDGs', *University World News,* 2 May 2010
http://www.universityworldnews.com/article.php?story=20100501081126465

MacGregor K and Makoni M (2010) 'Universities must be citadels not silos', *University World News, 2 May 2010*
http://www.universityworldnews.com/article.php?story=20100502103801345

Mamdani M (2008) *Scholars in the Marketplace: The dilemmas of neo-liberal reform at Makerere University 1989–2005*. Pretoria: HSRC Press

Moja T, Muller J and Cloete N (1996) Towards new forms of regulation in higher education: The case of South Africa. *Higher Education* 32(2): 129–155

Oyewole O (2010) Africa and the global knowledge domain. In: D Teferra and H Greijn (eds), *Higher Education and Globalization: Challenges, threats and opportunities for Africa*. The Netherlands: Maastricht University Centre for International Cooperation in Academic Development

Pillay P (2010a) *Higher Education and Economic Development: A literature review*. Cape Town: Centre for Higher Education Transformation

Pillay P (2010b) *Linking Higher Education and Economic Development: Implications for Africa from three successful systems.* Cape Town: Centre for Higher Education Transformation

Psacharopoulos G, Tan JP and Jimenez E (1986) *The Financing of Education in Developing Countries: Exploration of policy options.* Washington DC: The World Bank

Santiago P, Tremblay K, Basri E and Arnal E (2008) *Tertiary Education for the Knowledge Society. Volume 1.* Paris: Organisation for Economic Co-operation and Development

Sawyerr A (2004) *Challenges Facing African Universities: Selected issues.* Accra: Association of African Universities

Scott WR (2001) *Organizations: Rational, natural, and open systems.* Upper Saddle River, NJ: Pearson Education International

Sen A (1999) *Development as Freedom.* Oxford: Oxford University Press

Serageldin I (2000) University governance and the stakeholder society. Keynote Address, 11th General Conference: Universities as Gateway to the Future, Durban, 20–25 August 2000, International Association of Universities

Swartzman S (2010) *Changing Universities and Academic Outreach.* Rio de Janeiro: IETS

UNDP (1990) *Human Development Report 1990.* New York: United Nations Development Programme

UNDP (2009) *Human Development Report 2009. Overcoming Barriers: Human mobility and development.* New York: United Nations Development Programme

UNESCO (1998) World declaration on higher education for the twenty-first century: Vision and action. World Conference on Higher Education: Higher Education in the Twenty-First Century: Vision and Action. Paris, 9 October 1998

University of Botswana (2008) *University research strategy.* University of Botswana

US Congress (1994) *Higher Education in Africa: Hearing before the subcommittee on African affairs.* 17 May 1993. Washington: US Government Printing Office

WEF (2009) *The Global Competitiveness Report 2009–2010.* Geneva: World Economic Forum

WEF (2010) *The Global Competitiveness Report 2010–2011.* Geneva: World Economic Forum

Weick K (1976) Educational organisations as loosely coupled systems. *Administrative Science Quarterly,* 21:1–19

World Bank (1999) *Knowledge for Development. World Development Report 1998/99.* The World Bank Group. Oxford: Oxford University Press

World Bank (2002) *Constructing Knowledge Societies: New challenges for tertiary education.* Washington DC: The World Bank

World Bank (2009) *Accelerating Catch-up: Tertiary education for growth in sub-Saharan Africa.* Washington DC: The World Bank

Yesufu TM (ed) (1973) *Creating the African University: Emerging issues of the 1970s.* Ibadan: Oxford University Press

Appendix A

A higher education and development profile of the countries[14]

For many years, economic development was measured in terms of growth of gross domestic product (GDP). Long advocated by international agencies such as the World Bank during most of the second half of the 20th Century, this view argued that the sole concern of developing economies should be to generate high rates of economic growth, which would then permeate through a so-called 'trickle-down' effect to groups at the lower-end of the socio-economic ladder.

However, this rather narrow conception of economic development was broadened by the United Nations Development Programme (UNDP) to include human development and equity. In the *Human Development Report 1990,* human development was defined as 'the process of enlarging people's (basic) choices' (UNDP 1990). In subsequent Human Development Reports, the UNDP refined and extended the concept of 'human development' to include four basic components, of which the first is key – improved health, knowledge and skills – so that people can increase their productivity and participate fully in income-generation and remunerative employment.

From this emerged the Human Development Index (HDI) as a general measure of human development. The HDI is a composite of three basic components of human development: longevity, education and living standards. These components are expressed via the index of life expectancy at birth, the education index (measured by a combination of adult literacy and the combined gross enrolment ratio at primary, secondary and tertiary levels), and the GDP index (measured by real per capita GDP converted to US dollars or international dollars using purchasing power parity).

The human development perspective incorporates, to a large extent, the 'capabilities' approach' to development espoused by Amartya Sen (see Sen 1999, for example). Sen argues that in analysing social justice, there is a strong case for judging individual advantage in terms of the capabilities that a person has. In this perspective, poverty must be seen as the deprivation of basic capabilities rather than merely 'lowness of incomes', which is the standard criterion of identification of poverty. This perspective of capability does not involve any denial of the view that low income is clearly one of the major causes of poverty, and hence under-development, since lack of income can be a principal reason for a person's capability deprivation.

---

14   The bulk of this section was written by HERANA team member, Dr Pundy Pillay.

So what are the levels of growth in the sample countries, as expressed by GDP per capita? And, more importantly, to what extent has this growth been translated into human development?

Table A1 compares GDP per capita to the HDI for the eight African countries as well as the three international case study countries. The difference between the GDP per capita and HDI rankings is also calculated (last column). The difference between these two rankings reflects the divergence between economic and broader social development, and is often a consequence of inequality in access to income, education, health etc. For example, South Africa's HDI ranking is 51 places lower than its GDP per capita ranking, and Botswana's is 65 places lower – these figures are amongst the highest for the countries ranked in this report. Mauritius also exhibits a significant negative difference suggesting that equity may not be such a clearly defined outcome as the policies of the government imply. By contrast, in Finland and South Korea, the HDI ranking is greater than the GDP per capita ranking, suggesting a more holistic pattern of development with lower levels of social inequality. This is also true for Ghana, Kenya, Uganda and Tanzania but at much lower levels of development.

TABLE A1 **Gross domestic product (GDP) per capita vs. Human Development Index (HDI)**

Country	GDP per capita (PPP, USD)* 2007	GDP ranking	HDI Ranking (2007)**	GDP ranking per capita minus HDI ranking
Botswana	13 604	60	125	-65
Ghana	1 334	153	152	1
Kenya	1 542	149	147	2
Mauritius	11 296	68	81	-13
Mozambique	802	169	172	-3
South Africa	9 757	78	129	-51
Uganda	1 059	163	157	6
Tanzania	1 208	157	151	6
Finland	34 526	23	12	11
South Korea	24 801	35	26	9
United States	45 592	9	13	-4

Source: UNDP (2009)

Notes:

* PPP (purchasing power parity) shows a rate of exchange that accounts for price differences across countries, allowing international comparisons of output and incomes. In the table above, PPP USD 1 has the same purchasing power in the domestic economy as USD 1 has in the US.

** 177 countries were ranked.

Table A2 presents a selection of figures which highlight some aspects of the link between higher education and economic development. The most consistent correlation is between participation rate and stage of development; the higher the participation rate, the higher the stage of development. This shows at minimum that even if increasing participation rate is not a sufficient condition, it is at least necessary to change stage of development!

The table also shows that quality of schooling is important, with some exceptions. South Africa has the worst ranking of school quality, but nevertheless the highest competitiveness ranking of the African group – perhaps just another symptom of South Africa also having the highest GDP-HDI discrepancy. Kenya on the other hand has a quality of school system ranking much higher than South Korea and the US, but a very poor competitiveness ranking. The WEF ascribes this largely to weak institutional infrastructure (a code word for politics).

TABLE A2 Selected higher education and economic development indicators

Country	Stage of development (2009–2010)[1]	Quality of education system ranking (2009–2010)[2]	Gross tertiary education enrolment rate (2008)	Overall global competitiveness ranking (2010–2011)[2]
Ghana	Stage 1: Factor-driven	71	6.2[5]	114
Kenya		32	4.1[6]	106
Mozambique		81	1.5[3]	131
Tanzania		99	1.5[5]	113
Uganda		72	3.7	118
Botswana	Transition from 1 to 2	48	7.6[4]	76
Mauritius	Stage 2: Efficiency-driven	50	25.9	55
South Africa		130	15.44	54
Finland	Stage 3: Innovation-driven	6	94.4	7
South Korea		57	98.1	22
United States		26	82.9	4

Source: WEF (2010)

Notes:

[1] Income thresholds (GDP per capita in USD) for establishing stages of development (WEF 2010: 10): Stage 1 Factor-driven: <2 000; Transition from stage 1 to stage 2: 2 000–3 000; Stage 2 Efficiency-driven: 3 000–9 000; Transition from stage 2 to stage 3: 9 000–17 000; Stage 3 Innovation-driven: >17 000.

[2] Ranked out of 139 countries.

[3] 2005 figure.

[4] 2006 figure. The 2010 figure by the Botswana Tertiary Education Council is over 20% while in South Africa the figure remained around 16%.

[5] 2007 figure.

[6] 2009 figure.

The WEF defines 'competitiveness' as 'the set of institutions, policies, and factors that determine the level of productivity of a country' (WEF 2009: 4). The Global Competitiveness Index (GCI) is based on 12 pillars of competitiveness further divided into three pillar groups, which are:

- Basic requirements (institutions, infrastructure, macro-economic stability, health, primary education);
- Efficiency enhancers (higher education and training, goods market efficiency, labour market efficiency, financial market sophistication, technological readiness, market size); and
- Innovation and sophistication factors (business sophistication, innovation).

The GCI report regards higher education and training as an important factor in helping countries move towards a knowledge economy (WEF 2009: 5):

Quality higher education and training is crucial for economies that want to move up the value chain beyond simple production processes and products. In particular, today's globalising economy requires economies to nurture pools of well-educated workers who are able to adapt rapidly to their changing environment. This pillar measures secondary and tertiary enrollment rates as well as the quality of education as assessed by the business community. The extent of staff training is also taken into consideration because of the importance of vocational and continuous on-the-job training – which is neglected in many economies – for ensuring a constant upgrading of workers' skills to the changing needs of the evolving economy.

In 2007, the World Bank's report on the 'Knowledge Economy' identified three main messages. These included the following:

- Message 1: Knowledge and innovation have played a crucial role in development from the beginnings of human history. But with globalisation and the technological revolution of the last few decades, knowledge has clearly become the key driver of competitiveness and is now profoundly reshaping the patterns of the world's economic growth and activity. Both developed and developing countries should therefore think, with some urgency, 'about their future under a [knowledge economy] heading'.
- Message 2: To become successful knowledge economies, countries have to rethink and act simultaneously on their education base, their innovation systems, and their information and communication technology infrastructure, while also building a high quality economic and institutional regime. Policies for these four pillars have to reflect the country's level of development and will often have to be gradual. However, experience shows that some successful knowledge economy champions have been able to achieve spectacular leaps forward within a decade.
- Message 3: Many if not most of the countries that have made rapid progress have staged nationwide knowledge economy-inspired programmes of change. Such programmes have been pragmatic and country-specific, yet some common points emerge: the need to promote trust and social cohesion around the knowledge economy programme; the need to work at the four pillars through a combination of top-down reforms and bottom-up initiatives; and the need for a well-communicated knowledge economy vision.

Appendix B
List of interviewees

BOTSWANA

University of Botswana: Dr Dawid Katzke (Deputy Vice-Chancellor: Finance and Administration), Prof. Isaac Mazonde (Director: Research and Development), Prof. MB Khonga (Dean: Botswana College of Agriculture), Prof. B Tsie (Dean: Faculty of Social Sciences), Prof. Herman Batibo (UB-Tromso Basarwa Research Programme), Dr MMM Bolaane (UB-Tromso Basarwa Research Programme), Prof. B Chilisa (Principal Investigator: UB-UPENN HIV Study), Dr Jennifer Hays (UB-Tromso Basarwa Research Programme), Dr Kapunda (Department of Economics), Dr G Mookodi (Head: Department of Sociology), Prof. N Narayana (Acting Head: Department of Economics), Dr Gabo Ntseane (Head: Department of Adult Education), Mr EDM Odirile (UB Business Clinic, Faculty of Business), Prof. EK Quansah (UB Legal Clinic), Dr Wapula Raditloaneng (Department of Adult Education) and Prof. Siphambe (Department of Economics).

National stakeholders: Sebolaaphuti Kutlwano (Ministry of Finance and Development Planning) and Mr Richard Neill (Director: Policy and Planning, Tertiary Education Council).

GHANA

University of Ghana: Prof. Kwesi Yankah (Pro Vice-Chancellor), Prof. Esi-Sutherland-Addy (Institute of African Studies), Prof. Benjamin Ahunu (Provost: College of Agriculture and Consumer Science), Prof. Sam Offei (Associate Director: West Africa Centre for Crop Improvement), Mr Joseph Budu (Registrar: College of Agriculture and Consumer Science), Prof. Yaa Ntiamoah (Director: School of Research and Graduate Studies), Prof. Eric Danquah (Director: West Africa Centre for Crop Improvement), Dr Vernon Gracen (Associate Director: West Africa Centre for Crop Improvement), Prof. Kodjo Senah (Head: Department of Sociology), Prof. Isabella Quakyi (Principal Investigator: Gates Institute Partnership Projects for Population, Family and Reproductive Health), Prof. Alexander Nyarko (Director: West African Centre for International Parasite Control), Prof. Clement Ahiadeke (Deputy Director: Institute of Statistical Social and Economic Research), Dr Owuraku Sakyi-Dawson (Faculty of Agriculture) and Dr Esi Colecraft (Department of Nutrition and Food Science).

National stakeholders: Ministry of Education, National Council for Tertiary Education, Ministry of Finance and Economic Planning, National Development Planning Commission.

KENYA

University of Nairobi: Mr Ben Waweru (Academic Registrar), Prof. IM Mbeche (Principal: College of Humanities and Social Sciences), Prof. EHN Njeru (Dean: Faculty of Arts), Prof. Edward K Mburugu (Associate Dean: Faculty of Arts), Prof. Patts Odira (Dean: School of Engineering), Prof. Madara Ogot (Managing Director: University of Nairobi Enterprises and Services), Prof. Eric O Odada (Programme Director: Pan African START Secretariat), Prof. Dorothy McCormick (Institute for Development Studies), Mr John Njoka (Institute for Development Studies), Prof. Winnie Mitullah (Institute for Development Studies), Prof. NJ Muthama (Department of Meteorology), Prof. Francis Mutua (Hydrometrology and Surface Water Resources Unit), Prof. Njuguna Ng'ethe (Chronic Poverty Research Centre), Prof. John H Ndiritu (Dean: Faculty of Agriculture), Dr Wanjiru Gichuhi (Population Studies and Research Institute) and Mr Samuel W Kiiru (Institute for Development Studies).

National stakeholder: Elizabeth Wafula (Senior Assistant Commission Secretary (Planning): Commission for Higher Education).

MAURITIUS

University of Mauritius: Prof. I Fagoonee (Vice-Chancellor), Prof. Ameenah Gurib-Fakim (Pro Vice-Chancellor: Teaching and Learning), Prof. Soonil Rughooputh (Pro Vice-Chancellor: Research, Consultancy and Innovation), Prof. K Sobhee (Dean: Faculty of Social Studies and Humanities), Prof. T Bahorun (Department of Biosciences, Faculty of Science), Prof. D Jhurry (Department of Chemistry, Faculty of Science), Dr A Bhaw-Luximon (Department of Chemistry, Faculty of Science), Dr Dinesh Hurreeram (Department of Mechanical and Production Engineering, Faculty of Engineering), Mr I Koodoruth (Senior Lecturer: Department of Social Studies, Faculty of Social Studies and Humanities), Mr A Chutoo (Department of Computer Science and Engineering, Faculty of Engineering), Mr M Santally (Virtual Centre for Innovative Learning Technologies), Mr B Rajkomar (Senior Lecturer: Department of Agricultural Economics and Management, Faculty of Agriculture) and Dr V Ancharaz (Head: Department of Economics and Statistics, Faculty of Social Studies and Humanities).

National stakeholders: Mr Ricaud G Auckbur (Director: Post-secondary and Tertiary, Ministry of Education, Culture and Human Resources), Ms Maya Soonarane (Acting Director: Planning and Finance, Ministry of Education, Culture and Human Resources), Mr R Hittoo (Sector Ministry Support Team Leader for Education Empowerment: Ministry of Finance and Economic Empowerment), Dr Praveen Mohadeb (Tertiary Education Commission) and Mr S Rama (Principal Financial Analyst: Ministry of Finance and Economic Empowerment).

MOZAMBIQUE

Eduardo Mondlane University: Prof. Angêlo Macuacua (Deputy Vice-Chancellor: Management

Affairs), Prof. Orlando Quilambo (Deputy Dean: Academic Affairs), Dr Maria da Conceição (UEM Coordinator for SIDA/SAREC Cooperation), Dr Lidia Brito (Department of Wood Science and Technology), Dr Domingos Buque (Deputy Dean for Research and Postgraduation: Faculty of Education), Prof. António Cumbane (Head: Dept of Chemical Engineering), Prof. Amália Uamasse (Dean: Faculty of Science), Prof. Daniel Baloi (Dean: Faculty of Economics), Prof. Mário Falcão (Dean: Faculty of Agronomy), Prof. Armindo Ngunga (Director: Centre for African Studies), Prof. Manoela M Sylvestre (Director: School of Management and Entrepreneurship in Chibuto), Dr Álvaro Carmo Vaz (retired, Faculty of Engineering), Dr Afonso Lobo (Deputy Dean for Management: Faculty of Engineering), Prof. Boaventura Cuamba (Department of Physics), Prof. Serafina Vilanculos (Faculty of Engineering) and Prof. Brazao Mazula (Faculty of Education).

National stakeholders: Dr Venâncio Simão Massingue (Minister of Science and Technology), Constantino Gode (Advisor: Minister of Finance), Augusto Sumburane (National Director: Ministry of Finance Research Unit), Dr Vitória Afonso de Jesus (National Programme Coordinator: Programa Vilas de Milenio) and Dr Arlindo Chilundo (Advisor: Minister of Education and Culture).

SOUTH AFRICA

Nelson Mandela Metropolitan University: Prof. Derrick Swartz (Vice-Chancellor), Prof. Christo van Loggerenberg (Deputy Vice-Chancellor: Academic), Prof. Thoko Mayekiso (Deputy Vice-Chancellor: Research, Technology and Planning), Prof. Heather Nel (Director: Institutional Planning), Prof. Piet Naude (Director: Business School), Prof. Peter Cunningham (Head: Department of Sociology), Prof. Richard Haines (Professor: Development Studies), Prof. Hendrik Lloyd (Director: School for Economics, Development and Tourism), Ms Jackie Barnett (Director: Innovation, Support and Technology), Prof. Werner Olivier (Head: Department of Mathematics and Applied Mathematics), Prof. Danie Hattingh (Head: Automotive Components Technology Station), Ms Lucinda Lindsay (Researcher: Automotive Components Technology Station), Mr Andrew Young (Researcher: Automotive Components Technology Station), Prof. Hennie van As (Director: Institute for Sustainable Government and Development), Mr Xola Mkontwana (Centre Manager: Small Business Unit), Prof. Jan Neethling (Project Leader: Pebble Bed Modular Reactor project), Prof. Japie Engelbrecht (Project Leader: Pebble Bed Modular Reactor project), Prof. Ben Zeelie (InnoVenton, Institute of Chemical Technology), Geoff Ritson (InnoVenton Technology Support), Dr Willem van Heerden (Dept of Agriculture and Game Management), Prof. JJ van Wyk (Department of Building and Quantity Surveying) and Mr Hugh Bartis (Head: Department of Tourism).

TANZANIA

University of Dar es Salaam: Prof. MAH Maboko (Deputy Vice-Chancellor: Academic Affairs), Dr Sylvia Shayo Temu (Director: Planning and Finance), Prof. C Mwinyiwiwa (Acting Director: Research), Prof. FW Mtalo (Principal: College of Engineering and Technology), Dr Ulingeta Mbamba (Associate Dean: University of Dar es Salaam Business

School), Ms Katherine Fulgence (Business Development Service Incubation Programme), Dr AT Kamukuru (Faculty of Aquatic Sciences and Technology), Dr Cuthbert Kimambo (Business Technology Incubation, College of Engineering and Technology), Prof. NN Luanda (Dept of History, College of Arts and Social Sciences), Dr AE Majule (Institute of Resource Assessment), Dr Daniel Mkude (Department of Linguistics), Dr CL Nahonyo (Head: Department of Zoology), Dr Simon Ndaro (Kinondoni Integrated Coastal Area Management Programme, Faculty of Aquatic Sciences and Technology), Prof. James Ngana (Institute of Resource Assessment), Dr AK Temu (Tanzania Gatsby Trust, College of Engineering and Technology) and Mr Elia Yobu (Programme Officer: University of Dar es Salaam Entrepreneurship Centre).

National stakeholders: Wilbard Abeli (Director for Higher Education: Ministry of Education and Vocational Training), Fatima Kiongosya (Director of Planning: Ministry of Finance and Economic Affairs), Dr Bohela Lunogelo (Executive Director: Economic and Social Research Foundation), Mr Daniel Magwiza (Deputy Secretary: Grants, Finance and Administration, Tanzania Commission for Universities), Prof. MH Nkunya (Executive Director: Tanzania Commission for Universities), Denis Rweyemamu (REPOA – Research on Poverty Alleviation) and Grace Shirima (Ministry of Education and Vocational Training).

UGANDA

Makerere University: Dr Lillian Tibatemwa-Ekirikubinza (Deputy Vice-Chancellor: Academic Affairs), Prof. Eli Katunguka-Rwakishaya (Director: School of Graduate Studies), Mr JW Wabwire (Department of Planning and Development), Ms Florence Nakayiwa-Mayega (Department of Planning and Development), Prof. N Sewankambo (Principal: College of Health Sciences), Dr B Nawangwe (Dean: Faculty of Technology), Prof. Stephen Kijjambu (Dean: School of Medicine), Prof. Edward Kirumira (Dean: Faculty of Social Sciences), Dr Umaru Bagampadde (Head: Department of Civil Engineering), Prof. Sam Kyamanywa (Faculty of Agriculture), Dr Yasin Nakku Ziraba (Faculty of Technology), Ms Grace Twinamatsiko (Faculty of Technology), Dr Frederick Muyodi (Faculty of Science), Dr Joseph Byaruhanga (Uganda Gatsby Trust), Dr John Muyonga (Department of Food Science and Technology), Dr Dorothy Nakimbugwe (Department of Food Science and Technology), Dr Charles Niwagaba (Department of Civil Engineering), Dr Celestino Obua (Department of Pharmacology and Therapeutics), Dr Andrew Mwanika (Faculty of Medicine), Dr Leah Thayer (Infectious Diseases Institute), Prof. Richard Odoi (Department of Pharmacy) and Dr Juliet Kiguli (School of Public Health).

National stakeholders: Dr Evarist Twimukye (Economic Policy Research Centre, Ministry of Finance, Planning and Economic Development), Nyende Magidu (Economic Policy Research Centre, Ministry of Finance, Planning and Economic Development), Prof. ABK Kasozi (Executive Director: National Council for Higher Education), Ms Elizabeth Gabona (Commissioner for Higher Education: Ministry of Education and Sports), Mr Robert Odok Oceng (Visitation Committee to Public Universities, Ministry of Education and Sports), Mrs Rosseti Nabbumba Nayenga (Head of Poverty Desk: Ministry of Finance, Planning and Economic Development).

Appendix C

Indicators of pact, coordination and implementation

TABLE C1 **A role for knowledge and universities in development**

		3 = STRONG	2 = WEAK	1 = ABSENT
National	The concept of a knowledge economy features in the national development plan	Appears in a number of policies	Only mentioned in one policy document	Not mentioned at all
	A role for higher education in development in national policies and plans	Clearly mentioned in development policies		
Institutional	Concept of a knowledge economy features in institutional policies and plans	Features strongly in strategic plan and/or research policy/strategy	Vague reference in strategic plan or research policy	Not mentioned at all
	Institutional policies with regard to the university's role in economic development	Institutional policy	Embedded in strategic plan, research policy etc	No formal policies

TABLE C2 Coordination and implementation

		3 = SYSTEMATIC	2 = SPORADIC	1 = WEAK
COORDINATION				
National	Economic development and higher education planning are linked	Formal structures Headed by senior minister	Clusters/forums	Occasional meetings
	Link between universities and national authorities	Specific coordination structures or agencies	Some formal structures but no meaningful coordination	No structures, and political rather than professional networks
	Coordination and consensus building of government agencies involved in higher education	Higher education mainstreamed across government departments	Intermittent interaction with ineffective forums	Higher education issues limited mainly to one ministry or directorate
IMPLEMENTATION				
National	Role of the ministry responsible for higher education	Organised ministry with capacity to make predictable allocations	Spots of capacity with some steering instruments	Weak capacity with unpredictable allocations
		3 = STRONG	**2 = WEAK**	**1 = ABSENT**
	Implementation to 'steer' higher education towards development	Instruments such as funding or special projects that incentivise institutions/individuals	Occasional grants for special projects	No particular incentive funding
	Balance/ratio of sources of income for institutions	Government, fees and third stream	Mainly government plus student fees	Mainly government with external funders
	Funding consistency	A stable, transparent public funding mechanism based on criteria agreed upon by all actors involved	Funding allocations somewhat predictable but do not allow for long-term planning nor reward enterprising behaviour	No clear funding or incentives from government
Institutional	Specific units, funding or appointments linked to economic development	Specific units, funding or appointments	Economic development initiatives aspect of a unit or appointment	Mainly ad hoc, staff-initiated operations
	Incentives and rewards for development-related activities	Incentives or counts towards promotion	Some signals but largely rhetoric	No mention
	Teaching programmes linked to the labour market	Targets for enrolments in fields considered to be of high economic relevance	Some programmes in response to specific industry requests	No new programmes linked to labour market
	Special programmes linking students to economic development	Entrepreneurship, work-based learning and/or incubators for students mainstreamed	Ad hoc programmes	No special programmes
	Research activities are becoming more economy-oriented	Research policy/strategy has an economic development focus	Some research agendas have an economic development focus	Ad hoc project funding
	Levels of government and institutional funding for research	High	Medium	Low

Appendix D

Problems in collecting academic core data

Some universities could not extract the required data because they did not have appropriate or functional electronic student and staff data bases. In these cases, the data were only available in the form of summarised tables in print format. Where electronic data bases were in place, the data were often incomplete, classifications were inaccurate, graduate sets were incomplete, and not all marks used to indicate student success in specific courses had been captured.

A number of universities had no central management information office in which complete sets of the data were stored. In these circumstances data had to be collected directly from faculties or administrative departments. A consequence of this decentralisation was that different versions of data on students and staff were held by the university's various operational units. Because the focus of some universities was almost entirely on full-time student enrolments and their full-time staff establishment, their information on part-time students and part-time staff was poor and incomplete. The concepts of full-time equivalent students and full-time equivalent staff were not widely used. The data elements needed to make the necessary calculations were not available in a directly usable format in the case of most of the universities.

Copies of official documents such as annual reports and planning documents were brought back to South Africa and were used to check and correct the data on the CHET templates. Statistical reports found on the internet, as well as on the websites of the universities, were also used to check and correct data. Finally, where inconsistencies or gaps in the data or unusual trends were observed, the data were adjusted on the basis of analyses of average annual growth rates, and average ratios between data elements.

Appendix E

Academic core indicators and ratings

Table E1: Academic core indicators measurements and ratings

Indicators	Measurements	Ratings		
		Strong = 3	Medium = 2	Weak = 1
1 SET enrolments	SET enrolments as % of total enrolments: average for 2001–2007	% of enrolments in SET >39%	% of enrolments in SET between 30% and 39%	% of enrolments in SET <30%
2 Postgraduate enrolments	Masters and doctoral enrolments as % of total enrolments: average for 2001–2007	% of enrolments in masters plus doctors >9%	% of enrolments in masters plus doctors between 5% and 9%	% of enrolments in masters plus doctors <5%
3 Student–staff ratios	FTE academic staff to FTE enrolled student ratios: average for 2001–2007	Student to academic staff ratio <20	Student to academic staff ratio between 20 and 30	Student to academic staff ratio >30
4 Qualifications of academic staff	Proportion of permanent academic staff with doctorates: 2007 only	Permanent academic staff with doctorates >49%	Permanent academic staff with doctorates between 30% and 49%	Permanent academic staff with doctorates <30%
5 Availability of research funding	Research income per permanent academic staff member in purchasing power parity (PPP) dollars: 2007 only	Research funding per academic >ppp$20 000	Research funding per academic between ppp$10 000 and ppp$20 000	Research funding per academic < ppp$10 000
6 SET outputs	SET graduates divided by SET enrolments: average for 2001–2007	Ratio of SET graduates to SET enrolments >20%	Ratio of SET graduates to SET enrolments between 17% and 20%	Ratio of SET graduates to SET enrolments <17%
7 Knowledge production: doctoral graduates	Doctoral graduates as % of permanent academics: average for 2001–2007	Doctoral graduates in given year >10% of total permanent academic staff in that year	Doctoral graduates in given year between 5% and 10% of total permanent academic staff in that year	Doctoral graduates in given year <5% of total permanent academic staff in that year
8 Knowledge production: research publications	Research publications per permanent academic: average for 2001–2007	Ratio of 0.50 of publication units per permanent academic >0.50	Ratio of publication units per permanent academic between 0.25 and 0.50	Ratio of publication units per permanent academic <0.25

Lightning Source UK Ltd.
Milton Keynes UK
UKHW030706110220
358531UK00004B/367

9 781920 355807